ABOVE AND BEYOND

NASA'S JOURNEY TO TOMORROW

OLUGBEMISOLA RHUDAY-PERKOVICH

WITH INTRODUCTION FROM RORY KENNEDY

FEIWEL AND FRIENDS

NEW YORK

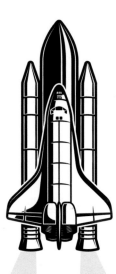

A Feiwel and Friends Book

An imprint of Macmillan Publishing Group, LLC

175 Fifth Avenue, New York, NY 10010

Our books may be purchased in bulk for promotional, educational, or business use. Please contact
your local bookseller or the Macmillan Corporate and Premium Sales Department at (800) 221-7945
ext. 5442 or by e-mail at MacmillanSpecialMarkets@macmillan.com.

Library of Congress Control Number: 2018936427

ISBN 978-1-250-30846-7 (hardcover) / ISBN 978-1-250-30847-4 (ebook)

Book design by April Ward

Feiwel and Friends logo designed by Filomena Tuosto

First edition, 2018

1 3 5 7 9 10 8 6 4 2

mackids.com

contents

INTRODUCTION

TONIGHT, LOOK OUTSIDE your window or maybe step outside your front door. Stand in your yard, on your sidewalk, on your street, and gaze up at the stars. Space is all around you—and for as long as humans can remember, women and men, girls and boys, have stood and stared up into the sky and wondered:

Where do we come from? Are we alone? What will become of us?

Six decades ago, on July 29, 1958, the National Aeronautics and Space Administration (NASA) set out to answer those questions and many more. It was a bold undertaking. As my uncle, President John F. Kennedy, noted when announcing the moonshot, we do these things "not because they are easy, but because they are hard, because that goal will serve to organize and measure the best of our energies and skills."

Our country was reaching out into the unknown with the hope of expanding human knowledge, on a mission to explore. And NASA sprung to life during an era of inspirational leadership—an agency that would represent the very best America had to offer and serve as a beacon for all the world.

Much time has passed since then, but certainly NASA's vigor and dedication have never wavered. In fact, part of the reason for publishing this book you are now holding, and for making the documentary that accompanies it, was to take stock—to pause and look back over the last sixty years and look forward to the next—to examine NASA's ongoing commitment to dreaming big and all that their dreaming has brought us.

Human beings have landed on the moon, built the International Space Station, and survived long-duration spaceflight. Robotic orbiters, landers, and rovers have toured the solar system, discovered water on Mars, and headed off into intergalactic space. Space telescopes have found billions of new galaxies and gazed back hundreds of millions of light-years in time.

There is so much NASA has done and so much we now know because of NASA—and tomorrow promises even more. The Space Launch System aims to make humans an interplanetary species; the James Webb Space Telescope hopes to show us the origins of the universe; the Mars 2020 Rover may enable us to bring back a piece of Mars. These are truly heroic endeavors, and the astronauts, scientists, engineers, and many others who are carrying out these missions are true heroes.

And in all this, in all these pages filled with courageous feats, amazing discoveries, and inspiring individuals, what has been for me the most important lesson?

The simple truth that the more we look out, the further we journey into space—be it by rocket ship, satellite, or telescope—the more we learn about our own planet. This is, after all, where the title of my film and this book is derived—for just as NASA travels *beyond*, so, too, it watches from *above*. As much as we have set our sights on space, we do so on behalf of Earth.

Ours is an extraordinarily unique planet. To date, we have found no other planet quite like it. We have found no other planet with life and no other planet capable of sustaining life.

NASA presently has over 19 different satellites studying the Earth. Along with aircraft and ground teams, the agency directly measures almost every aspect of our planet's environmental systems. From melting ice caps to scorching wildfires, from dying coral reefs to parched farmlands, from thawing permafrost to rising coastal waters—all that information has been streaming in over days, years, and decades to give us a comprehensive global view of our very complicated planet.

And this is as vital as anything NASA has ever done. It is data we share with the world—data that has taught us all about the reality of climate change.

So, if you are looking out your window or perhaps standing in your yard, maybe your eyes are turned upward and you are gazing out at all those billions of stars, it is my belief that the most important thing the universe can teach us is about ourselves.

Where do we come from? Are we alone? What will become of us?

NASA continues to explore.

—RORY KENNEDY

CHAPTER ONE

IT'S ON

ON DECEMBER 17, 1903, Wilbur and Orville Wright made the United States the "first in flight" when they produced the first successful powered airplane. In freezing-cold weather, Orville Wright was airborne for 12 seconds and flew a total of 120 feet. The Americans had rockets. They had airplanes. The United States was ready to soar.

"Not so fast," said other countries around the world. They wanted to get up, up, and away, too. And they did. By 1914, several European countries had passed the US in the development of airplane technology.

The race was on.

IT IS ROCKET SCIENCE, ACTUALLY

Used as a military weapon for centuries, rockets—or "fire arrows" as they were once called—were originally fueled by gunpowder and had an impact reflected in the noise they made, which was described as "thunder." As a teenager, Robert Goddard became fascinated by rockets after reading about them in H. G. Wells's now-classic science-fiction story, *The War of the Worlds*. Goddard began designing rockets himself, wondering how they could be made to travel to even greater heights. At the same time, a Russian teacher named Konstantin Tsiolkovsky was trying to

solve the same problem. It wouldn't be the last time an American and a Russian would be in this situation.

Both came to the conclusion that a space-bound rocket would need liquid fuel, which was more powerful. Goddard went on to design and build rockets and suggested that one could be flown to the Moon. He was ridiculed for this proposal and kept his ideas to himself after that. But he kept on thinking and building, and on March 16, 1926, he flew one of his own rockets a distance of about 152 feet—the very first liquid-fueled rocket flight in known history.

Europe continued to develop its own interest in rocketry. German engineer Hermann Oberth wrote a book in 1923 titled *The Rocket into Planetary Space*. Many read Oberth's work and dreamed of spaceflight; a teenager named Wernher von Braun did a little more than dream.

Von Braun went on to work with Oberth and then with the German Army during World War II, developing rockets for research—and as weapons. He refined his liquid-powered rockets, fueled by ethanol and liquid oxygen, and developed the A4 (or V-2) rocket, which was first launched on October 3, 1942. This successful send-off of a ballistic missile is said to be the start of the Space Age.

As World War II ended, von Braun, who had been a member of the Nazi party, surrendered to American soldiers and was brought to the US. Von Braun and his colleagues set up shop once again and went on to develop the Mercury-Redstone rockets, which launched astronauts Alan Shepard and Gus Grissom on the United States' first suborbital flights. The Mercury-Redstone rockets also launched the Pioneer 1 satellite—NASA's first spacecraft—and later they launched John Glenn's historic trip around Earth's orbit.

naca: TESTING OUR LIMITS

On March 3, 1915, Congress created the National Advisory Committee for Aeronautics (NACA). The committee was a small team of volunteers and one employee named John F. Victory. Would his last name be a sign of things to come?

The NACA was an independent government agency that reported directly to the US president. It conducted flight tests throughout the 1910s and 1920s and developed a research facility (Langley Memorial Aeronautical Laboratory). By 1925, the team had grown to include more than 100 employees. The NACA helped develop faster and stronger aircraft. It also worked on simplifying the designs used in World War II aircraft and in the first supersonic airplane (in a partnership with the US Air Force and the Bell Aircraft Corporation). The NACA went on to study missile technology and began to explore the possibilities of sending humans on the ultimate thrill ride—to space. In July 1950, the Bumper 2 was the first rocket launched from Cape Canaveral in Florida. It reached an altitude of almost 250 miles, which was a record at the time.

PLANE/ROCKET, TOMATO/TOMAHTO . . . NOT QUITE

Airplanes are able to fly because air moves along their wings, working in opposition to the pull of gravity and giving them *lift*. But that only works at relatively low altitudes. High in the sky, the atmosphere is too thin to hold an airplane up. Rockets, however, don't care about that. Rockets are powered by their own fuel, which pushes them up à la Newton's third law of motion: For every action, there is an equal and opposite reaction. Rockets have a fuel tank and an oxygen tank; the two combine to burn the fuel that powers the rocket. Rocket engines push gases down, so the rocket goes up.

Sputnik means "fellow traveler" in Russian.

The Cold War between the United States and the Soviet Union (USSR) was a period of increased tension and competition between the two world powers that got serious after World War II; by the 1950s, the "space race" was on. In the battle between West and East, each side was determined to demonstrate its superior strength and technological advancements. On October 4, 1957, the Soviet Union launched Sputnik 1, the first man-made satellite to enter Earth's orbit.

President Eisenhower officially congratulated the Soviets a few days later, but the pressure was on. On October 14, the American Rocket Society proposed the development of a new agency, one that focused on research and developments in outer space that were not related to military defense. Americans believed themselves to be great explorers, and if space was the new frontier, then they were going to get in on the game.

But the Soviets continued to blaze ahead. Less than a month after the launch of Sputnik 1, the USSR sent Sputnik 2, the first vehicle carrying a living being, into space—the cosmonaut was a former stray dog named Laika.

Meanwhile, many in science and government felt that the NACA wasn't enough. The US needed something more or, better yet, something new. President Eisenhower proposed legislation to Congress to establish a National Aeronautics and Space Agency, and on July 29, 1958, the National Aeronautics and Space Act was signed into law. Along with it, the National Aeronautics and Space Administration (NASA) was born.

Unfortunately, the Sputnik 2 mission was a sad one; Laika died a few hours after blasting off, probably from overheating and panicking in the unfamiliar and challenging environment.

Is there such a thing as *inner space*? *Outer space* (or just *space*) is anything outside the Earth's atmosphere, which is officially defined as any distance beyond 100 kilometers (60 miles) from Earth's surface. So *inner space*, which is not really a thing except for in a 1987 sci-fi comedy film, could be considered the atmosphere within our orbit.

PROFILE: Eilene Galloway

Eilene Galloway, a congressional researcher and consultant, suggested *administration* instead of *agency* because she thought it sounded like it had more authority, and an administration would be able to coordinate the activities of various related agencies. People were less likely to mess with an administration. Galloway, who was often called "the Grande Dame of Space," was very influential in national and international space policy. When she was first asked by Senator Lyndon B. Johnson to help with the congressional hearings that led to the development of NASA, she wasn't exactly sure that she was the right person for the job. "The only thing I knew about outer space at that time," she said, "was that the cow had jumped over the Moon."

But she went on to become an expert, helping to write treaties that governed international space-exploration activity. She was opposed to using space and space technology in warfare and was a large part of the creation of the International Institute of Space Law, which studies the legal issues surrounding space exploration. Trained as a performer and debater and known as a witty storyteller, Galloway was indispensable to government at home and abroad. The American Institute of Aeronautics and Astronautics gave her its highest honor in 2006, naming her an honorary fellow. She also received the first Lifetime Achievement Award from Women in Aerospace and was honored by NASA for her work advising Congress, the United Nations, and more. Eilene Galloway died in 2009, two days before her 103rd birthday.

HOW IS NASA ORGANIZED?

NASA is an independent civilian (not military) agency of the executive branch of government. It was created by Congress, and Congress must approve all its budget and legislation matters. NASA headquarters are in Washington, DC. The big boss—the NASA administrator—works there. NASA also has components around the world, including ten flight and research centers located around the United States. There are also three Deep Space Network (NASA's telecommunication system) facilities located in the United States, Spain, and Australia.

When we think of NASA, the first thing we usually think of are astronauts. But there are 18,000 people who work at NASA, and they do all kinds of jobs. "Scientists at NASA include oceanographers, geologists, agricultural scientists, scientists who study glaciers and ice sheets, and climate scientists, to name just a few," says former NASA Chief Scientist Ellen Stofan. "But there are also all kinds of engineers who build spacecraft and instruments, and astronauts who observe Earth from space. But NASA also has lawyers, accountants, and doctors. If you think of a profession, one expert probably works at NASA!"

NASA GODDARD SPACE FLIGHT CENTER
GREENBELT, MARYLAND

"Don't let anyone tell you that you cannot do it. And don't do something simply because someone tells you that you should do it. You have to find what you're good at and what you really enjoy doing."

—Mamta Patel Nagaraja, aerospace engineer

PROFILE: MAMTA PATEL NAGARAJA

San Angelo, Texas, where Mamta Patel Nagaraja grew up, might not seem like the typical breeding ground for future astronauts. "For a young girl from a small town in a largely underserved area, getting to NASA was pretty much unheard of," she said in an interview. But while some older siblings can specialize in being bossy, Nagaraja's older sister helped spark an interest in science, leading Nagaraja and her siblings in science experiments and showing them articles and newspaper clippings of science-related news. Nagaraja also got an early start in developing engineering skills by working with power tools and appliances in a small motel run by her parents, who remain a source of inspiration. Encouraged by some special educators in her life, she went on to earn three degrees in three different subjects: an undergraduate degree in aerospace engineering, a master's degree in mechanical engineering, and then a doctorate degree in biomedical engineering. She went on to work in a variety of ways for NASA at the Johnson Space Center, training astronauts to operate the space shuttle and working as a flight instructor. Nagaraja currently runs the Women@NASA program, connecting children to the past and present women who have played a variety of roles at NASA. Her NASA GIRLS and NASA BOYS virtual mentoring program allows children all over the country to interact with real NASA employees doing all kinds of different jobs. "Today, I get to communicate science—the awe-inspiring science that delves into the universe in a quest to know the unknown," she says. "I challenge myself daily to frame that science in ways that people can relate to it and know the impact it has on their own lives."

what exactly is an engineer, anyway?

Many of the people at NASA, from astronauts to food scientists to educators, are engineers. So what exactly does an engineer do?

Engineers are often considered problem-solvers, builders, inventors, dreamers, and makers. Engineers generally design solutions to problems in daily life—in NASA's case, on Earth and in space! They look for ways to develop systems that improve society. "As an engineer, you might develop the next generation of the iPad, or a medical device that will help doctors treat an illness, or a spacecraft that will carry humans to Mars, or a system that can bring clean water to an underdeveloped region, or a new power source that is sustainable and provides clean energy, or a device that can detect toxic agents and chemicals, or a new building that is earthquake-safe," says TryEngineering.org. There are many kinds of engineers, including electrical, mechanical, civil, biomedical, computer, environmental, chemical, and, of course, aerospace. Chances are that if there's a problem you want to solve in the world, engineering can help you do just that!

BLASTOFF

NASA kickstarted space exploration in the US with the January 1958 launch of its first satellite, Explorer 1. Explorer 1 measured the radiation in Earth's orbit and returned data that eventually demonstrated that Earth was circled by radiation belts, which are named Van Allen belts after the scientist who discovered

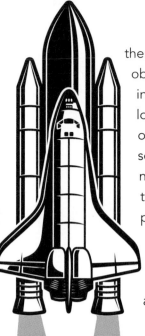

them. Explorer 1 was the first orbital object to bring science instruments into space. That was soon followed by the launch of Pioneer 1 on October 11, 1958. NASA selected its first group of astronauts in 1959. Those chosen had to have experience with jet airplanes and training in engineering and had to be less than 5 feet 11 inches tall. Seven military men became NASA's first astronauts.

The US was doing big things.
And secret things.

During the Cold War, the US government was increasingly concerned about the possibility of a nuclear attack from the USSR. In 1995, long before Google Maps, it was revealed that a satellite called Corona had been developed by the CIA, the military, and businesspeople to spy on military operations in regions of the USSR. In 1960, Corona was the first vehicle to successfully collect film images from space—which showed that the USSR didn't have the nuclear capabilities that it said it did.

WHAT—OR WHO, FOR THAT MATTER— WERE WE EXPECTING FROM SPACE TRAVEL?

While the 1940s and '50s saw serious, high minded conversation about space exploration and new frontiers, there were other conversations happening on the ground, too—ones about "little green men" and giant women called "Amazons." *Little green men* became common terminology for aliens, perhaps as successors to trickster fairies and leprechauns of folklore. Harold Lawlor's 1946 story published in *Weird Tales* magazine, "Mayaya's Little Green Men," is the first-known usage of the term in science fiction. In addition to being small and vegetable-colored, aliens were depicted as annoying and rude in Frederic Brown's rather unfriendly 1955 novel, *Martians, Go Home.* But the Mariner 2's flyby of Venus in 1962 proved everyone wrong.

"Venus was a mysterious planet," says NASA historian Bill Barry. "It's shrouded in clouds. It's hot. And other than that, we didn't know a whole lot about it." Perhaps because it was named after the goddess of love, our nearest planetary neighbor, Venus, was often imagined to be inhabited by beautiful, angry women, as shown in the 1958

film *Queen of Outer Space.* The Mariner 2 showed us that no women, angry or not, could have survived on that planet—it was beyond just "hot." "I remember reading books about it as a kid," says Barry. "[The books said] 'You know, it's got all these clouds. It's probably very wet. Venus is this jungle planet' . . . So in 1962, Mariner 2 goes flying by Venus, and we find out that not only is Venus a lot hotter than we thought, but it was so hot that nothing could live there."

Though US space exploration reassured NASA and the government that Russia was not on the brink of leading the nation to nuclear war, there were other things going on in the Eastern bloc. On April 12, 1961, Russian cosmonaut Yuri Gagarin became the very first human in space, orbiting the earth in Vostok 1. Less than four years after launching Sputnik 1, it looked like Russia had won the space race. By a lot.

FUN FACT "I'm coming back in . . . and it's the saddest moment of my life." These words were spoken by Edward H. White, who was the first US astronaut to take a spacewalk on June 3, 1965. White, who was pilot of the Gemini 4, enjoyed his spacewalk so much that he didn't really want to return to the aircraft! Gemini 4 also made another mark, leaving behind one of the first pieces of "space junk" when, like many of us, the team lost a glove—it flew out through the open hatch and into space, where it floated until the atmosphere burned it up about a month later!

TO THE MOON . . . AND BACK

"We set sail on this new sea because there is new knowledge to be gained, and new rights to be won, and they must be won and used for the progress of all people. For space science, like nuclear science and all technology, has no conscience of its own. Whether it will become a force for good or ill depends on man, and only if the United States occupies a position of pre-eminence can we help decide whether this new ocean will be a sea of peace or a new terrifying theater of war."

—President John F. Kennedy, "We choose to go to the Moon" speech, September 12, 1962

"Let both sides seek to invoke the wonders of science instead of its terrors. Together let us explore the stars, conquer the deserts, eradicate disease, tap the ocean depths, and encourage the arts and commerce," said President Kennedy in his 1961 inaugural address. That sounds nice and friendly, but make no mistake, the space race was still *on*.

Playing a game of catch-up, NASA's Project Mercury, the first US program dedicated to putting humans in space that had been established near the end of 1958, took center stage. Project Mercury sent its first American, Alan Shepard, into space on May 5, 1961, on a 15 ½-minute flight that went 116 miles into the air. Appealing to Congress, President Kennedy announced a new goal—sending humans to the Moon and then bringing them back safe and sound. Kennedy reportedly held out hope that the space program could be a vehicle for cooperation between the United States and Soviet Union, but he ultimately held firm that "this is, whether we like it or not, a race." NASA's budget was increased significantly. The country was shooting for the Moon.

John Glenn became the first American to orbit Earth in 1962. He went around three times and spent about five hours in space.

4ᶜ U.S. MAN IN SPACE
PROJECT MERCURY

ASTRONAUTS

While the names Shepard and Glenn are among the most well-known, there were actually seven men chosen to be NASA's first space travelers. Called "astronauts" after the Argonauts of Greek legend and the pioneers of balloon travel, these men might have seemed average. They were highly trained test pilots and engineers who underwent rigorous assessments before being allowed to take a spacewalk. Each endured a week of medical and psychological evaluations, 30 different laboratory examinations, physical endurance exercises, and more. "In addition to pressure-suit tests, acceleration tests, vibration tests, heat tests, and loud-noise tests, each candidate had to prove his physical endurance on treadmills, tilt tables, with his feet in ice water, and by blowing up balloons until exhausted," reports NASA. The men went through continuous psychiatric evaluation and even had to live with psychiatrists. They took

While Kennedy and Khrushchev were hardly best buds, there were some areas of cooperation in their orbits. A popular Soviet space dog named Strelka had a puppy named Pushinka that Khrushchev gifted to the Kennedys. Pushinka met a Kennedy dog named Charlie, and the two of them had four puppies that JFK called "pupniks"!

personality tests that required they answer questions like, "Who am I?" NASA psychologist and researcher Robert Voas explained: "The purpose of the testing program at Wright Field was to determine the physical and psychological capability of the individual to respond effectively and appropriately to the various types of stresses associated with space missions." Those first seven—Carpenter, Cooper, Glenn, Grissom, Schirra, Shepard, and Slayton—went on to become American space celebrities, but foremost they were brave volunteers committed to advancing the cause of space exploration.

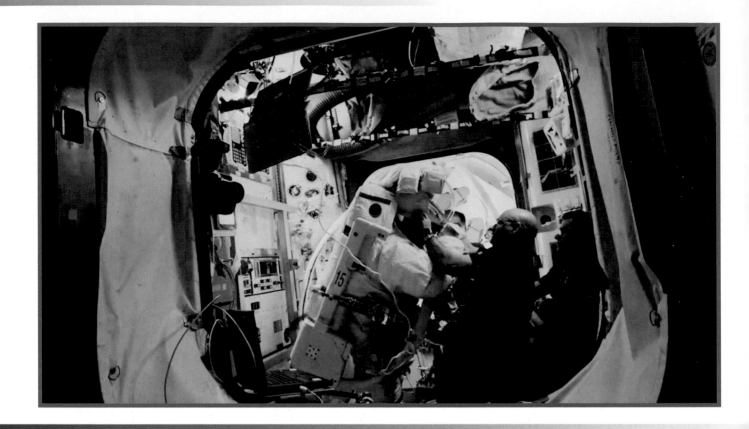

THE GIMBAL RIG MERCURY ASTRONAUT TRAINER

It looked like an amusement-park ride and probably felt a bit like one, too. The gimbal rig was used to test the effects of spinning on the body. Astronauts sat inside three aluminum cages that simulated the tumbling movements that could be expected in space travel. The cages could revolve together or separately, tossing the astronauts around at a speed of up to 30 revolutions per minute. The seven Project Mercury astronauts trained on the gimbal rig for five hours each; soon after, 13 women, known as the Mercury 13, did the same.

THE GALLAUDET ELEVEN

Before the US could send humans into a zero-gravity environment, they had to understand the effects of long-term exposure to that environment. NASA recruited eleven deaf men, nicknamed the Gallaudet Eleven (they came from what is now Gallaudet University), whose inner ear damage made it so that they never experienced motion sickness. The men—Harold Domich, Robert Greenmun, Barron Gulak, Raymond Harper, Jerald Jordan, Harry Larson, David Myers, Donald Peterson, Raymond Piper, Alvin Steele, and John Zakutney—spent over a decade undergoing testing and experiments in many different conditions and environments. One test involved sailing in very rough waters off the coast of Nova Scotia, Canada. The Gallaudet Eleven played cards and relaxed, but the researchers got so sick that the experiment had to end! Once, four of the Gallaudet Eleven spent 12 days inside the "Vomit Comet"—a 20-foot, constantly revolving room that offers a roller coaster–like experience of weightlessness. You might guess the reason why it got that name. The work of the Gallaudet Eleven went a long way toward our understanding of the human body's adaptation to space travel. They were instrumental in the development of the US space program.

Since the Gallaudet Eleven demonstrated that living with deafness didn't prevent them from being able to withstand the conditions of space travel, will the United States ever send a deaf astronaut into space? If it's up to Julia Velasquez, the answer will be a resounding "YES." A Gallaudet University graduate, Velasquez was a NASA intern and is now a researcher, trained crisis counselor, and human-rights advocate. As the 2017 winner of the #StudentAstronaut competition, she's already had a taste of what it might be like to live as an astronaut on Mars. She spent time living in the Mars-like HI-SEAS habitat in Mauna Loa, Hawaii. "As the first deaf #StudentAstronaut, I aim to share with the world that we are a thriving community, rich in culture and language," she said, using American Sign Language in an interview with *Xploration Station*. "This will send a powerful message on the importance of inclusivity in science and space exploration."

In his historic "We choose to go to the Moon" speech at Rice University on September 12, 1962, President Kennedy proclaimed that "those who came before us made certain that this country rode the first waves of the industrial revolutions, the first waves of modern invention, and the first wave of nuclear power, and this generation does not intend to founder in the backwash of the coming age of space. We mean to be a part of it—we mean to lead it." Kennedy was talking about living out dreams and achieving the fantastic; he knew well that this commitment to space exploration was "an act of faith and vision."

a new perspective/
THE GREAT ADVENTURE

Project Apollo was first established by NASA under President Eisenhower as a three-astronaut follow-up to Project Mercury's one-man jaunts into space. But later, President Kennedy's goal of landing a human being on the Moon became NASA's first priority. While many were interested in "beating" the Soviet Union, the larger purpose of scientific exploration and discovery was what made the idea exciting to others. "This was really exploration at its finest," said astronaut Jim Lovell, who was on the crew of two of the most famous Apollo missions, 8 and 13.

The Apollo missions had a bumpy beginning, including a tragic preflight fire on January 27, 1967, onboard what became known as Apollo 1. Edward H. White, the man who took the first spacewalk; Gus Grissom; and Roger Chaffee lost their lives. Two days later, Flight Director Gene Kranz addressed his brokenhearted team: "Space flight will never tolerate carelessness, incapacity, and neglect. Somewhere, somehow, we screwed up. It could have been a design in build or in test, but whatever it was, we should have caught it . . . From this day forward, Flight Control will be known by two words: *tough* and *competent*. Tough means we will forever be accountable for what we do or what we fail to do. We will never again compromise our responsibilities. Every time we walk into Mission Control, we will know what we stand for . . . When you leave this meeting today, you will go to your office, and the first thing you'll do is write *tough and competent* on your blackboards. It will never be erased. Each day when you enter the room, these words will remind you of the price paid by Grissom, White, and Chaffee."

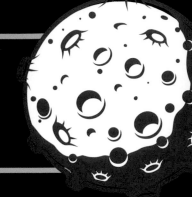

"Near the end of his presidency, Kennedy returned to the idea of super-power cooperation in space," reports NASA. "Speaking before the United Nations on September 20, 1963, he proposed 'a joint expedition to the Moon' and asked, 'Why should man's first flight to the Moon be a matter of international competition?'"

LUNAR MODULES MADE APOLLO MOON LANDINGS HAPPEN IN A COOL, VOLTRON-LIKE WAY

When President Kennedy announced his plan to land a human being on the Moon by the end of the 1960s, NASA scientists had a real challenge. There wasn't exactly a spacecraft that could get someone there . . . yet. Hypothetically, they could try to build a supersize rocket—but that would be too hard to build and it was too expensive to even try. But NASA had some existing technology that made a way possible—it created a three-part system called "Lunar Orbit Rendezvous." First, there was the Saturn 5 rocket, which would get things going with the big blastoff at launch. Docked into the Saturn 5 were 1) the command/service module (CSM), which was made up of two parts: the command module was the control center, to hold the crew and equipment needed to return to

Earth, and the service module provided engine power and storage capabilities for oxygen and fuel for breathing and drinking; and 2) the lunar module (LM), which was the piece that would detach from the whole contraption and land on the Moon. Lightweight (by space standards), it was designed to hold two astronauts, take them to the Moon, hang out in the Moon's orbit while they walked around, then deliver the astronauts and whatever goodies they were bringing back to Earth to the CSM. The LM could not function in Earth's atmosphere—only outside of it. So after the crew was transferred back to the CSM, the LM would be separated from the rest of the parts and sent back out into orbit. The Apollo 11 mission was the first to use this system successfully.

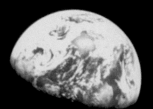

DRESSED OUT OF THIS WORLD

The 1960s might have been the height of space-age excitement, though much of the fascination with space travel and futurism began much earlier. The ideas of exploration and pushing boundaries were present in much of pop culture, from the popularity of rocket toys and "outer space–theme Tupperware parties" to architecture like "Boytopia," a clubhouse design sponsored by the Boys' Club of America in the '50s. Boytopia was meant to be "an extravagant playground for future generations who would play with radar, solar energy, atomic batteries, and spacecraft engines." *Popular Science* reports that Boytopia's design included "an aircraft work area and shops, television and radar labs, a football stadium with a foldable plastic roof, and an observation tower." Leslie Greener's 1951 science-fiction novel *Moon Ahead* impressed with sound rocket science principles on top of its thrills. Movies like *12 to the Moon* and *20 Million Miles to Earth* were on theater screens around the country, and '60s cars got sleeker, designed with rocket-like qualities. But one field took the space-age concept to new heights—and lengths: fashion.

Sometimes called "the father of space-age couture," André Courrèges incorporated his background in engineering and architecture into his fashion designs. Joel Lobenthal writes that "his dresses, suits, and trouser suits might be fitted, semi-fitted, or tubular, but they present a bold and graphic silhouette." Even NASA took note of Courrèges's interest in space and invited him to visit mission control at Cape Canaveral. Courrèges went on to design La Bulle, an early electric car, along with cameras, robots, and motor scooters.

Paco Rabanne, a fashion designer also trained as an architect, was very interested in the use of hard materials as body coverings. He designed the costumes for the sci-fi film *Barbarella*, which "created a sensation in 1968 with ready-to-wear sheaths of plastic squares and discs attached to fabric backing."

Fashion designer Pierre Cardin offered yet more space age–inspired creations with his vinyl, silver, giant zippers and hard, helmet-like visors. He also came up with a menswear line called Cardin's "Cosmonaut" collection.

Apollo 7 was the first mission that successfully brought a US crew into space (and possibly the only one where the commander, Walter Schirra, yelled "Yabba dabba doo!" like Fred Flintstone, the cartoon character). The spacecraft lifted off on October 11, 1968, and a few minutes in, Commander Schirra reported that "she is riding like a dream." It wasn't the most comfortable trip; going to the bathroom, especially for number twos, meant undressing to use "defecation bags" that, despite being sealed up and stored away after use, were pretty smelly. And the crew caught colds less than 24 hours into the flight, which can be annoying enough when you have to stay home in bed. In space, where you're weightless, it means that it's a pain to try to get snot out. The nasal passages don't drain, and blowing your nose really hard also really hurts. But despite some challenges and discomforts, Apollo 7 was a success and set the stage for the next mission.

Then Apollo 8 changed everything.

1968 had seen much turmoil. The cost of and opposition to the Vietnam War had intensified. Civil-rights leader Martin Luther King Jr. was brutally assassinated; uprisings in several cities followed.

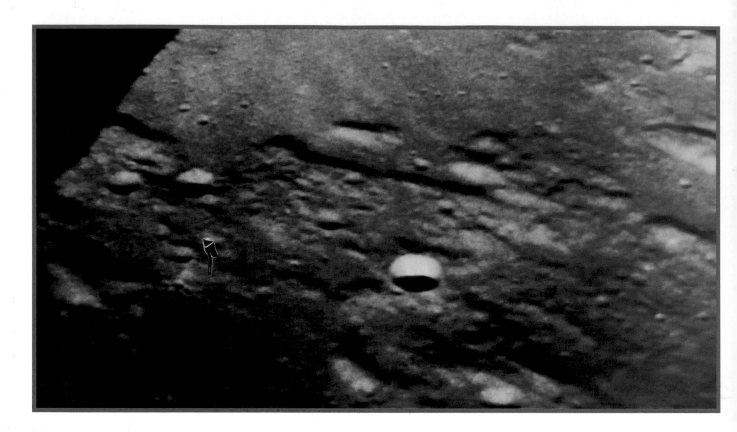

Senator Robert F. Kennedy—who was the president's brother, the former attorney general, and a US presidential candidate—was killed. Many Americans were demanding change on the ground. And, as always, NASA scientists wondered what they might find in the skies.

Apollo 8 was meant to *circumnavigate*, or go around, the Earth to test the lunar module, but the LM wasn't quite ready for that yet. Still, the pressure from Russia was on, and the United States did not want to continue their game of playing catch-up. "So NASA thought," says Lovell, who was the Apollo 8 navigator, "maybe we should send Apollo 8 to circumnavigate the Moon." The Apollo 8 crew of Lovell, William Anders, and Commander Frank Borman blasted off on December 21, 1968. Lovell says that the 240,000-mile trip took three days. As they traveled around the Moon, marveling over its craters, astronaut William Anders took a now-legendary photo of the Earth. That photo, known as *Earthrise*, was the very first image of Earth captured by a human being from outer space. "Suddenly everybody could see the Earth as it truly is: a grand oasis in the vastness of space," says Lovell. Millions around the world watched and listened as the astronauts shared images of the Earth and Moon along with their thoughts on the experience of seeing our planet from another perspective. "'We came to explore the Moon,'" Lovell remembers Anders saying, "'and we discovered the Earth.'"

On Christmas Eve, Apollo 8 entered Lunar orbit. NASA had instructed the astronauts to "do something appropriate" to mark the occasion. They ended up reading the first ten verses from the Biblical book of Genesis. On Christmas morning, as they began their journey back to Earth, Lovell also reported back, "Roger, please be informed there is a Santa Claus."

"To be sure, we are behind and will be behind for some time in manned flight. But we do not intend to stay behind, and in this decade, we shall make up and move ahead . . . Many years ago, the great British explorer George Mallory, who was to die on Mount Everest, was asked why did he want to climb it. He said, 'Because it is there.'

"Well, space is there, and we're going to climb it, and the Moon and the planets are there, and new hopes for knowledge and peace are there. And, therefore, as we set sail, we ask God's blessing on the most hazardous and dangerous and greatest adventure on which man has ever embarked."

—President John F. Kennedy, "We choose to go to the Moon" speech, September 12, 1962

On July 20, 1969, with over half a billion people around the world watching, Neil Armstrong walked on the Moon. Upon taking his first steps, he proclaimed the now-legendary words, "That's one small step for man, one giant leap for mankind." Fellow Moon voyager astronaut Buzz Aldrin described the Moon's landscape as "magnificent desolation." After exploring the Moon's surface for a couple hours, the Apollo 11 team left behind "an American flag, a patch honoring the fallen Apollo 1 crew, and a plaque . . . It reads, HERE MEN FROM THE PLANET EARTH FIRST SET FOOT UPON THE MOON. JULY 1969 A.D. WE CAME IN PEACE FOR ALL MANKIND."

Just over a year after his "We choose to go to the Moon" speech, President Kennedy was assassinated on November 22, 1963. The NASA center that would launch the Moon voyagers was named in his honor: the Kennedy Space Center in Florida. On July 20, 1969, when the crew of Apollo 11 landed on the Moon, a bouquet of flowers was placed on the Kennedy gravesite at Arlington National Cemetery. The note read, *Mr. President, the Eagle has landed.*

The Apollo 11 crew had done it: They had landed on the Moon and come back to Earth. With its talk of "tessering" through space and time, Madeleine L'Engle's novel *A Wrinkle in Time* had been too unimaginable for the more than 25 publishers who'd rejected it; that changed after Apollo 11. *A Wrinkle in Time* went on to win the Newbery Award in 1963. That was the same year that President Kennedy launched the Apollo Program. The stuff of science fiction was reality.

Many of the over 500 million who watched the Apollo 11 mission on television probably wondered: *On what fantastic voyage will NASA take us next?*

The answer was: home.

"The vast loneliness is awe-inspiring, and it makes you realize just what you have back there on Earth." —Jim Lovell, NASA astronaut

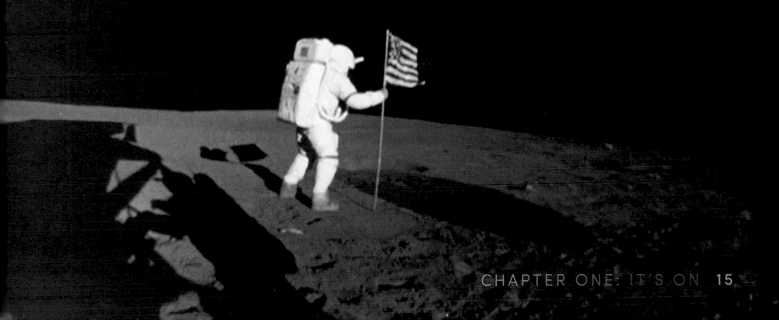

CHAPTER TWO

A LOOK IN THE MIRROR

I'M OKAY, YOU'RE OKAY: HOW SPACE EXPLORATION TAUGHT US ABOUT HOME

AFTER THE EXHILARATING DAYS of 1960s Moon fever, President Richard M. Nixon took a more pragmatic approach as a new decade began. "We must also recognize that many critical problems here on this planet make high-priority demands on our attention and our resources," he said in a statement about the future of the US space program in March 1970.

In other words: *Settle down, moonwalkers. We've got stuff to do here at home.* Though the Apollo Program had been largely seen as successful, President Nixon decided that there would be no more special treatment—from now on, NASA would be treated as less of a special, separate entity and more like just another domestic policy area and would have to compete for the same federal funding as other government agencies.

Maybe it wasn't a surprise. After all, Nixon reportedly clapped and said "Hooray" when Neil Armstrong took his first steps on the Moon.

Nixon wanted to refocus NASA's priorities to be more in line with domestic needs, and to look at ways to apply space technology to technological innovation at home. He said:

"We must think of [space activities] as part of a continuing process . . . and not as a series of separate leaps, each requiring a massive concentration of energy. Space expenditures must take their proper place within a rigorous system of national priorities . . . What we do in space from here on in must become a normal and regular part of our national life and must therefore be planned in conjunction with all of the other undertakings which are important to us."

NASA's budget was cut, and the end of the Apollo Program was scheduled. Though Nixon's plans may have seemed to put a damper on the enthusiasm for the space program, he was the first president to attend a space launch (Apollo 12), and in 1972, he did usher in an important new development: the Space Shuttle program. This new type of space vehicle would be more like a reliable and reusable family car, offering quick and lower-cost transportation to carry humans. Nixon imagined its uses to be both civilian and military; perhaps space shuttles would be helpful during natural disasters like earthquakes, and it was reported that he thought they might be useful in the disposal of nuclear waste.

Now that the Moon race had been "won" (at least from the US point of view), Nixon was also interested in increased international cooperation when it came to space. While celebrating the Apollo 11 Moon landing, Nixon spoke with astronauts Buzz Aldrin and Neil Armstrong on the phone. "As you talk to us from the Sea of Tranquility, it inspires us to redouble our efforts to bring peace and tranquility to Earth."

The Soviets seemed to agree. "The Soviet and American spacemen will go up into outer space for the first major joint scientific experiment in the history of mankind," said Soviet leader Leonid Brezhnev. "They know that from outer space, our planet looks even more beautiful. It is big enough for us to live peacefully on it, but it is too small to be threatened by nuclear war."

Both countries had also endured space-program tragedies: the memories of Apollo 1 were still fresh in US minds, and cosmonaut Vladimir Komarov, the pilot of the Russian Soyuz 1, had been killed in 1967 due to a series of spacecraft malfunctions.

HOUSTON, WE'VE HAD A PROBLEM.

Meant to be NASA's third Moon landing, the Apollo 13 flight has become legendary. Crew and Ground Control managed to avoid tragedy when the spacecraft lost oxygen and power over 200,000 miles away from Earth.

Apollo 13 launched on April 11, 1970, with the usual crew of three: Jim Lovell, Fred Haise, and Jack Swigert. Swigert was a backup crew member who was called in at the last minute when original team member Ken Mattingly was exposed to measles. This type of last-minute replacement was challenging; astronaut teams work together for long periods before their missions, developing trust. But the Apollo 13 crew went with the flow. They had no choice.

The trip's first couple of days were uneventful. "The spacecraft is in real good shape as far as we are concerned. We're bored to tears down here," said Ground Control team member Joe Kerwin at about 47 hours in. A few minutes later, the astronauts broadcast a live demo of their life and work in a "weightless" environment, and after almost an hour, Jim Lovell wished the world good night. "This is the crew of Apollo 13 wishing everybody there a nice evening, and we're just about ready to close out our inspection of Aquarius and get back for a pleasant evening in Odyssey. Good night."

A few minutes later, there was "a loud bang."

An oxygen tank had exploded onboard the command module (CM).

Then another one failed, and that meant that the electricity, water, and power supply were lost. With the bang and warning light sending a frightening message, Swigert famously told Ground Control: "Houston, we've had a problem here."

The three transferred from the CM to what was now the "lifeboat"—the lunar module—which they would use to travel back to Earth. The problem was that they had to get back before the supplies that kept them alive ran out. The LM itself was built to last for 45 hours, but they'd need it for 90. They had to conserve power and water. "They cut down to six ounces of food and drink each per day—one-fifth of normal intake—and had fruit juices; they ate hot dogs and other wet-pack foods when they ate at all. The crew became dehydrated and set a record that stood up throughout Apollo: Lovell lost 14 pounds, and the crew lost a total of 31 $\frac{1}{2}$ pounds, nearly 50 percent more than any other crew." Without the electrical systems, it was also very cold. "The temperature dropped to 38 degrees Fahrenheit, and condensation formed on all the walls."

They also had to manage the removal of carbon dioxide from the LM. "The LM was designed to support two men for two days and was being asked to care for three men for about four days." Carbon dioxide levels also rose to dangerous heights. Mission Control on the ground helped the crew jerry-rig a temporary solution. Before the explosion, Apollo 13 had been on a lunar landing course. Now it was time to literally switch gears, mid-voyage, and figure out a course back home. The LM navigation system wasn't equipped for this, so the astronauts and ground crew had to work together to figure things out on the spot. The usual procedure of using an alignment optical telescope for star navigation was impossible; because of the explosion, debris had made stars too hard to see. Ground Control came up with a system of using the Sun for navigation and guided Jim Lovell to turn the craft in the right direction.

NASA has records stating that while Flight Director Gerald Griffin seemed to have kept his cool, he was anything but.

He said, "Some years later I went back to the log and looked up that mission. My writing was almost illegible, I was so damned nervous. And I remember the exhilaration running through me: *My God, that's the last hurdle—if we can do that, I know we can make it.* It was funny, because only the people involved knew how important it was to have that platform properly aligned."

PIONEER 10
JUPITER PROBE

Later, all Griffin coolly said was: "That check turned out real well."

Incredibly, flight controllers took only three days to figure out a way to power up the CM again—a process that normally took three months.

With the world watching, on April 17, Apollo 13 landed safely in the South Pacific Ocean, about three and a half miles from the USS *Iwo Jima*.

Haise, later remembering the emotions of the flight, was disappointed. "Our mission was a failure . . . I mean, there was no way around it. There's no question it was a remarkable recovery from a bad situation. But at the same time, relative to the mission intended, it was a failure."

Lovell says he thinks of it as more of an unexpected opportunity. "We were given the situation . . . to really exercise our skills and our talents to take a situation [that] was almost certainly catastrophic and come home safely. That's why I thought that 13, of all the flights—including [Apollo] 11—that 13 exemplified a real test pilot's flight."

In the 1995 film *Apollo 13*, Ed Harris, playing lead Flight Director Eugene F. Kranz, says, "We've never lost an American in space; we're sure as hell not going to lose one on my watch. Failure is not an option."

Though many believe that these exact words were the ones uttered on the mission, they were not. Kranz suspects they were inspired by a speech he made while trying to keep the team's spirits up. "I said, 'This crew is coming home. You have to believe it. Your people have to believe it. And we must make it happen,'" recalls Kranz. Kranz liked the film's paraphrase, though, and used it as the title of his autobiographical book in 2000. Flight Controller Jerry C. Bostick says that he was asked by the filmmakers how Ground Control all remained calm during what seemed like certain disaster. "In preparation for the movie, the script writers . . . came down to Clear Lake to interview me [and asked] 'What are the people in Mission Control really like?' One of their questions was 'Weren't there times when everybody, or at least a few people, just panicked?' My answer was 'No. When bad things happened, we just calmly laid out all the options, and *failure was not one of them*. We never panicked, and we never gave up on finding a solution.'"

Like the main thing that made the safe return of the Apollo 13 crew possible, it sounds like Ed Harris's line in the film was inspired by some extraordinary teamwork.

THE GHOST SHIP

Though it seemed like the government's appetite for space travel had cooled a bit, there were some major voyages, including one that was truly outer space–bound: the unmanned travels of Pioneer 10. Before 1972, Americans hadn't ventured too far out beyond flying by nearby planets like Mars and Venus, moon-walking, and doing research in the general inner–solar system neighborhood. But on March 2, 1972, Pioneer 10 was launched on a mission to get past the "bands" of Jupiter . . . and it did. By achieving *escape velocity*, or enough speed to escape Earth's atmosphere, Pioneer 10 was used to study the asteroid belt around Jupiter, Jupiter's environment, and farther corners of our solar system than we'd ever seen before. It went on toward Saturn's orbit in 1976, Uranus's three years later, and Neptune's in 1983. Pioneer 10 was built to last; an engineer involved in its construction reportedly commented that "this spacecraft is guaranteed for two years of interplanetary flight. If any component fails within that warranty period, just return the spacecraft to our shop, and we will repair it free of charge." It lasted two years and then some, gathering data that was crucial in the construction of the Voyager and Galileo spacecraft and setting humans on track for exploration of the outer solar system. A final, very weak but still detectable signal was received by the Deep Space Network from Pioneer 10 on January 23, 2003, more than 30 years later. It's still out there; NASA calls it a "ghost ship" that "will continue to coast . . . through deep space [and] into interstellar space." Pioneer 10 will head generally for the giant orange star Aldebaran, which forms the eye of the constellation Taurus. Aldebaran is about 68 light-years away. It will take the ghost ship over two million years to reach it.

THE VOYAGER SPACECRAFT

Launched in 1977, Voyager 1 and 2 have now traveled far beyond Pluto, farther than anything else from Earth. Voyager 1 discovered Jupiter's active volcanoes. Voyager 2 is the only spacecraft to have visited Uranus and Neptune. Right now, Voyager 1 is NASA's "fastest and farthest" spacecraft and the only object made by humans that is out in *interstellar space*, or the area that lies beyond the solar wind, magnetic field, and gravitational pressure of our Sun, where the pull is stronger from the mass that's in between the stars. Both Voyager 1 and 2 carry golden records (they're actually gold-plated copper) that have recorded sounds and images of Earth on them—just in case they are recovered by other complex life-forms.

VOYAGER 1

The recordings include natural sounds like thunder, wind, birds, and whales, as well as different types of music, greetings in a variety of languages (from ancient Akkadian to Wu, a Chinese dialect), and printed messages from President Carter and United Nations Secretary General Kurt Waldheim. Noted astronomer Carl Sagan worked with a team to develop the plan for the records. The packages include protective aluminum casings, cartridges, and needles, along with symbols indicating instructions for playing the records. NASA points out that it will take about 40,000 years for either Voyager to leave our solar system. "The spacecraft will be encountered and the records played only if there are advanced spacefaring civilizations in interstellar space," pointed out Sagan. "But the launching of this bottle into the cosmic ocean says something very hopeful about life on this planet."

Though E.T., the extra-terrestrial from the 1982 film of the same name, really couldn't have used a public pay phone to "phone home," he might have had luck with NASA's Deep Space Network. There are three groups of antennae at ground stations located in California's Mojave Desert as well as in Madrid, Spain, and in Canberra, Australia. They're in these three spots around the world so that as the Earth rotates, at least one will be able to communicate with any satellite in deep space. As you might guess, they are HUGE: The antennae diameters range from 111 to 230 feet.

THE FIRST US SPACE STATION: SKYLAB

For a large portion of the 1970s, NASA ran the Skylab Program, which launched the Skylab space station. It is the United States' first (and still only) space station. Rocket-science master Wernher von Braun had been dreaming of one since the '50s; the idea was included in a series of articles that he helped put together called "Man Will Conquer Space Soon!" (The articles later became the basis for a book series and episodes of the television series *Disneyland*.) It was fitting that the last mission of one of von Braun's Saturn V rockets launched the unmanned Skylab 1 into orbit.

Other parts of the Saturn V were recycled and used in the construction of Skylab 1. NASA points out that "turning a rocket into a laboratory was not easy, but it was an affordable way to build a space station, because existing hardware could be used," and affordability was a big plus for '70s NASA programs. Skylab was built to include a workshop, where the crew could live and work, and a solar observatory that applied Apollo technology to observe and record previously unavailable data about the sun.

Going out into space and hanging out for a while was a new idea. In fact, the third Skylab crew set a record when it spent 84 days in space. (Valeri Vladimirovich Polyakov holds the current record for the longest stay in space; he was on the Mir Space Station for 437 days and 18 hours.) And spending that time conducting complicated science experiments was revolutionary. The Skylab project proved that astronauts could live and work together in a microgravity environment for long periods of time. And those of us who suffer from cabin fever know that that's a really big deal! From May 25, 1973, to February 8, 1974, three crews of three astronauts went to Skylab, carrying out 270 experiments in physics, astronomy, and biology.

Skylab got off to a rocky start, though. Sixty-three seconds into its launch, a solar shield ripped off, causing the spacecraft to lose electrical power and putting Skylab at risk of overheating. The first crew (Skylab 2) was sent up to repair the damaged spacecraft, but their work was made even more challenging by a communications blackout. When the lines of communication reopened, Mission Control (and the world!) heard a few words that they probably weren't meant to hear. "The astronauts were venting their frustration with four-letter words, while Houston repeatedly tried to remind them that [public] communication had resumed," NASA reported. The crew made the repairs successfully, ultimately demonstrating even more of what's possible to accomplish in space.

Skylab 3, the second manned mission, extended the medical research conducted by the first crew. For instance, they'd seen that the Skylab 2 mission caused "puffy-face syndrome" for the crew. Puffy-face syndrome is a side effect of zero-gravity space travel—without the effects of Earth's gravity, blood and fluid fills a human's head, making the face and upper body swell. The Skylab 3 crew gathered pre-flight and inflight data during its mission to learn more about the condition. Skylab 3 also had a larger crew than the first mission.

Skylab 4, the third and final mission, was made up of a crew of space rookies—none of them had been in space before. This crew, which launched on November 16, 1973, spent Thanksgiving in space. They had their choice of meals: Commander Gerald Carr had prime rib, William Pogue had chicken and gravy, and Edward Gibson went old-school with a turkey dinner. NASA reports that "as earlier crews had done, the third crew reported that the food was very good but slightly bland." Because they were on a strict astronaut diet, they couldn't use much salt, and they couldn't have a ginormous Thanksgiving meal. For the most part, they ate well—though sometimes bits of food flew out of its packaging and floated around the lab!

These were long missions in very tight spaces. And sometimes the astronauts didn't take kindly to being bossed around by people enjoying the wide expanses and comforts of planet Earth. "Skylab's third crew in particular complained repeatedly about being overloaded with tasks and superhuman expectations," explains writer Elizabeth Howell. After some talks between the ground crew and the astronauts, things went smoothly, and the team went on to accomplish even more than had been planned.

The Skylab crew enjoyed many opportunities to observe our planet on their extended voyage. NASA

Model of orbital space station Skylab

historians have a record of the astronauts' reactions. "One awed astronaut could only exclaim 'Holy cow!' as he watched the lights of Acapulco, Guadalajara, and then Mexico City brilliantly greet them through the clear, cold, December sky. Then, as they passed over the Texas coast, they could see clearly from Brownsville to Port Arthur, then New Orleans, and, finally, the entire eastern United States, with lights aglow from the Great Lakes to the Gulf."

Carr said, "It's like a spiderweb with water droplets on it." The crew also took thousands of photos of Earth from space, including an accidental one of Area 51, the top-secret United States Air Force Facility that has long been the subject of many rumors.

MULTISPECIES CREW

Along with some mice, fruit flies, and single-celled organisms, a couple of "arachnauts" came along for the ride—two spiders named Anita and Arabella. Because spiders use their own weight to determine the thickness of their webs, a high schooler named Judy Miles wondered if spiders could spin webs in a weightless environment, also called *microgravity*. NASA thought that was a good question! So they brought the spiders along. After a couple of days, Arabella got the hang of space and spun a web that was similar to one she'd have created on Earth. Anita, who had some extra time to figure things out while Arabella worked, spun a decent web a little more quickly when it was her turn. Both webs were a little finer than the ones they would have spun on Earth, but they were still webs! This was very helpful to scientists studying the effects of microgravity on motor control. The spiders died before the voyage ended; their bodies are preserved at the Smithsonian National Air and Space Museum in Washington, DC.

Apollo 17 was the very the last Apollo mission, launched on December 7, 1972. Liftoff occurred after midnight; because of a minor technical issue, it was delayed and remains the only nighttime launch of a NASA manned spacecraft. It was also the last time NASA astronauts left low-Earth orbit. The crew on this lunar exploration mission was sent to gather information about a "highly varied" site on the Moon. Apollo 17 astronaut Harrison "Jack" Schmitt remembers, "We had three dimensions to look at with the mountains, to sample. You had the mare basalts in the floor and the highlands in the mountain walls. We also had this apparent young volcanic material that had been seen on the photographs and wasn't immediately obvious, but ultimately we found [it] in the form of the orange soil at Shorty Crater.

"But as soon as you had a chance to look around, you could tell—everything we expected to find there, and more, was going to be available to us, and that's what geologists like. And they really like to have the unexpected . . . you get a new surge of adrenaline when you find there are things that you never could have anticipated. And that's discovery. That's when science really becomes exciting, those things that you didn't anticipate and they occur, and that's where scientific discoveries are made."

THE LAST MAN ON THE MOON

On December 14, 1972, Commander Eugene A. Cernan took the last human steps on the Moon's surface:

> "Bob, this is Gene, and I'm on the surface. As I take man's last steps from the surface, back home, for some time to come, but we believe not too long into the future. I'd like to just list what I believe history will record: that America's challenge of today has forged man's destiny of tomorrow. And, as we leave the Moon at Taurus-Littrow, we leave as we come and, God willing, as we shall return, with peace and hope for all mankind. God-speed, the crew of Apollo 17."

Astronauts on '60s space missions like Mercury, Gemini, and Apollo had gotten some great shots of our planet from space. Remember William Anders's *Earthrise* photo? That was big. This final Apollo mission, Apollo 17, provided us with another iconic image of our planet: *Blue Marble*. It is considered one of the most widely-known images of space ever. It reminded us that the Earth was a small, fragile planet, just one object in the middle of the vastness of space, "alone in the universe" in many ways.

This new perspective on Earth had an enormous impact on the way we live now.

THE INTERNATIONAL SPACE HANDSHAKE: APOLLO-SOYUZ

One of the biggest signals that the space race had officially ended was the Apollo-Soyuz project. The plan sounded like something out of science fiction: NASA astronauts in an Apollo vehicle would literally have a space meetup with Russian cosmonauts in a Soyuz capsule. The two countries would even collaborate on the design of a docking mechanism that both capsules could use. Just the idea of this was a radical departure from the WrestleMania-style attitudes of the past. "We thought they were pretty aggressive people and . . . they probably thought we were monsters," said NASA Commander Module Pilot Vance Brand in an interview, whose first space voyage was the Apollo-Soyuz test flight.

"The purpose of the mission . . . was, as I see it, twofold. One, it was to test the docking system, a unique new piece of hardware different from docking systems we had used in the past . . . and the other purpose was international relations. It was, 'How do we take two space programs that grew up from separate roots and coordinate them, make them work together?'"

Rather than the back-and-forth game of one-upmanship and trash-talking that characterized the 1960s, the United States and the Soviet Union decided to commit to the policy of *détente*—a French word that means "relaxation." In other words, they were going to chill for a bit. And what better place to do that than in space? But there was much to overcome.

Each country's space vehicles were built very differently. Astronauts had a considerable amount of control of the cone-shaped Apollos, while spherical Soyuz spacecraft relied much more on mechanical navigation. Somehow, they had to connect to the same docking station in space, which was kind of like trying to charge an iPhone and an Android phone from the same charger. You can see a model of the docked Apollo-Soyuz configuration at the Smithsonian National Air and Space Museum in Washington, DC. Even the air the two crews breathed was different: In order to maintain oxygen supply, Soyuz capsules used a mix of nitrogen and oxygen in their atmospheres, while Apollos had a pure-oxygen environment.

And there was the little matter of communication. Space travel was downright dangerous, requiring split-second decision-making. Communicating in different languages could leave a lot of room for error. The solution: Each team learned the other's language and spent time in the other's country, getting to know the culture. In an interview with NASA, Commander Thomas P. Stafford remembered, "We were trying to converse, and it just wasn't—we just weren't . . . I said, 'Look, I'll speak Russian to you, and you speak English to me. Maybe we can understand it better.'" So, the USSR cosmonauts spoke to the American astronauts in English, and the American astronauts replied in Russian. "Boy, it worked slick as a whistle."

Vance Brand said, "It was useful to talk in their language and for them to talk in ours, in that case, because everyone tended to slow down and be more careful in what they said. We all thought communication would be better in case of an emergency or something like that." It was a great way to practice *and* be on an even playing field of sorts. "When you deal with people that are in the same line of work as you are, and you're around them for a short time, why, you discover that, well, they're human beings," said Brand. Later USSR cosmonaut Aleksei Leonov joked that there was actually another language spoken: "Oklahomski." Stafford, born and raised in Oklahoma, had a particularly difficult time with the Russian language, which became a running joke.

There was a near-tragedy for the Apollo-Soyuz crew just before landing back on Earth: The crew was accidentally exposed to toxic nitrogen gas. The astronauts choked, and Brand was briefly unconscious. After a safe landing, the three astronauts were hospitalized, but all of them recovered.

Differences notwithstanding, both the USSR and the US were committed to a joint project, and in 1972 they signed the "Agreement Concerning Cooperation in the Exploration and Use of Outer Space for Peaceful Purposes," which agreed to the launch of the Apollo-Soyuz lab three years later.

On the NASA side, there was a three-man crew: Stafford, Brand, and Donald Slayton. The Soviets went with two: Leonov and Valeri Kubasov. The Soyuz 19 capsule launched seven hours before the Apollo. On July 17, 1975, the two rendezvoused and docked in the newly engineered station that could accommodate a Soviet spacecraft on one side and a NASA model on the other.

A global television audience watched as the astronauts and cosmonauts met in the docking module and shook hands. For a couple of days, the teams worked together on experiments, exchanged gifts, shared meals, practiced docking and redocking, and broadcast live from space. The crews sent messages directly to President Gerald Ford and Soviet Premier Brezhnev. The Soyuz returned to Russia on July 21; the Apollo stayed up a few days longer, conducting experiments.

> "We have succeeded.
> Everything is excellent."
> —Thomas Stafford, Apollo Commander

The mission was a success. It was the last time that an Apollo spacecraft would be used for space travel and was a precursor to later projects such as the Mir and ISS.

After the Apollo-Soyuz mission, the United States would not send another human being into space for five years. But NASA was doing plenty in the meantime.

LANDSAT

Though the Pioneer and Voyager crafts were gathering data from the more-distant planets, NASA was always keeping an eye on conditions back home. And that was a good thing, too, for all of us.

In 1965, the US Geological Survey (USGS) suggested that since we'd had some success with gathering weather information from weather satellites, why not do something similar to collect data about

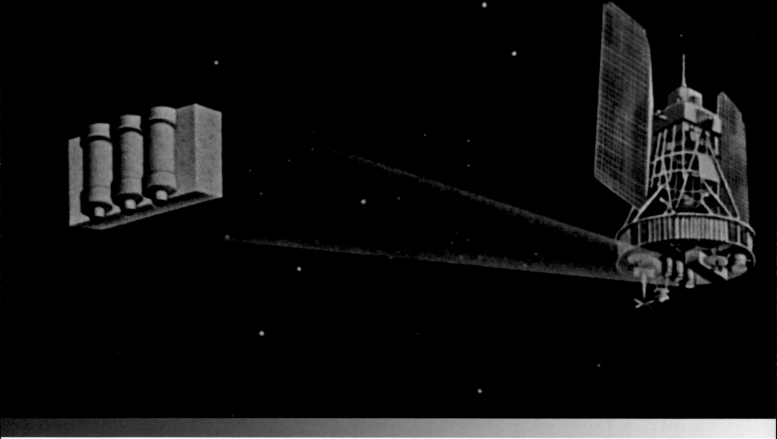

our own terrain? All of NASA's fancy space equipment might even create some important reuse-and-recycle opportunities. NASA historian Bill Barry says scientists were thinking, "'We've got all these instruments that provide scientific data about other planets . . . We could use those instruments and put them into orbit around Earth and look at Earth!'"

Whoa, whoa, whoa, said the government officials with their eyes on our country's wallet. *Satellites sound a little pricey.* Some wondered how we would get permission to take photographs of other countries. The Department of Defense worried that US military scouting missions might be compromised.

But other branches of government got the ball rolling, and in 1970, NASA got the go-ahead for the world's first Earth-observing satellite program. Landsat 1 launched on July 23, 1972, as a joint USGS/NASA project. "It's a really significant development, and it could only be done because of space exploration," says Barry.

Landsat satellites (they were originally—and less smoothly—named Earth Resources Technology satellites) measure and gather data from the Earth's surface. This helps us see exactly how our land and natural resources change, how human activity affects our water, air quality, wildlife . . . everything. Landsat 1 was fully loaded with a

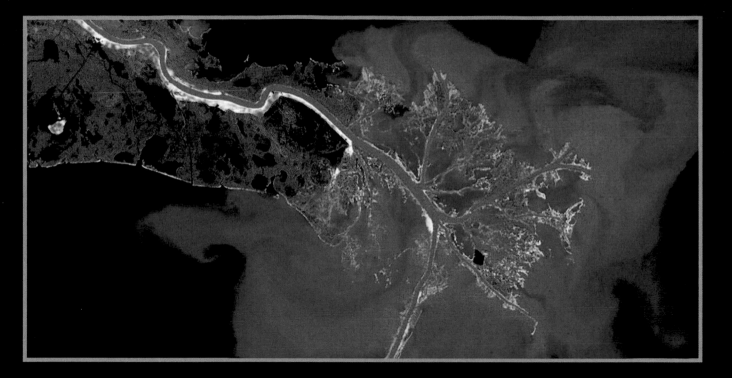

camera system called RBV and a multispectral scanner (MSS). The RBV was supposed to be the big dog, but it was the MSS that turned out to be extremely useful. It showed images of the Earth in four brightly colored wavelengths—red, green, and two infrared bands. This method of imaging allowed for accurate views of the land that we live on—about 30 percent—and, of that percentage, what we use—approximately 80 percent. More than 300 researchers worked together to analyze the data, including scientists in a variety of disciplines from all over the world. Not only did Landsat allow us to see and learn new things, it became a system that continues to do that over time. By 2022, the Landsat program will have been operating for 50 years, and there's no sign of it slowing down.

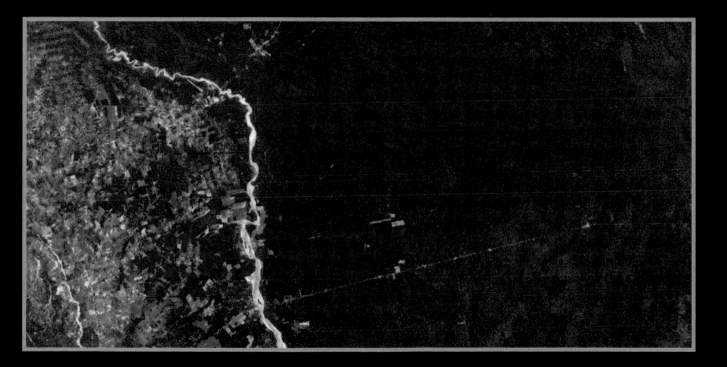

MAKING DATES WITH DATA

How exactly does a satellite like Landsat send information back to scientists? Beams of light? Dots and dashes? Brain waves? Email?

Satellites send two types of data back to researchers. First there's the "housekeeping" data, which is information about the craft itself—how it's working, its traveling path, etc. Then there's the science-y stuff, the information that it was sent out into space to collect. This information is stored on the satellite and then sent to a central location via telemetry—that means it's sent via wireless systems, like radio signals, infrared technology, telephone, or computer networks. These systems can organize data and send it in batches over great distances, so there's no "info dump" of complicated data. Satellite antennae send radio signals to antennae on Earth, where the information is stored on computers at an antennae facility. Then the data is transmitted to an operations center, which sends it along to a data-processing center that sorts and translates all of the different kinds of data into a format that the researchers understand.

"It's being able to go back in time for the same location, with the same program, that's given us a tremendous amount of really valuable information . . . With Landsat we can do that because the archive is so rich." —Alan Belward, scientist

You and your family probably benefit from Landsat regularly. Landsat data helps us identify potential environmental health risks, analyze crop health, and plan recovery efforts after natural disasters. Google finds Landsat useful, too. Chris Herwig, a Google geo data engineer, paid tribute to the now middle-aged Landsat on its forty-fifth birthday: "Over the years, we've used the Landsat imagery to develop an incredibly accurate depiction of Earth and its changes over time, which we've published in Google Earth and Maps for use by billions of people worldwide."

Scientists around the world work together to use Landsat to track the development of cities and the changes in our climate, as well as to figure out how we will continue to live on Earth. Data from Landsat is used in many areas, including human health, energy, urban growth, water management, ecosystems and biodiversity, and forest management.

Landsat was groundbreaking in the way that it facilitated NASA's commitment in working with other nations to observe our planet and share data. "In 1975, NASA Administrator James Fletcher predicted that if one space-age development would save the world, it would be Landsat and its successor

satellites," NASA recorded. And in the 1980s, it was this type of research and analysis of our planet that basically saved us from ourselves.

LINGERING DREAMS OF GALAXIES FAR, FAR AWAY

The "space opera" *Star Wars* opened in movie theaters in 1977, and with it came a renewed interest in worlds and galaxies beyond our own, and new dreams of humans living in and exploring the outer reaches of the universe.

What else happened in 1977? The first space shuttle orbiter, the Enterprise, made its first flight tests.

Gene Roddenberry, the creator of *Star Trek*, as well as many of the cast members attended the dedication ceremony. The Enterprise shuttle is currently on view at the Intrepid Sea, Air & Space Museum in New York City. While the USS Enterprise would "boldly go where no man has gone before" every week, the space shuttle Enterprise was not built to go into space. It did, however, pave the way for the space shuttle program that characterized the next decade.

FUN FACT The Enterprise was originally going to be named the Constitution. But hardcore Trekkers (or Trekkies, depending on who you ask), aka fans of the TV series *Star Trek*, successfully petitioned then-President Gerald Ford to name it after the spacecraft on the show, the USS Enterprise.

CHARON (MOON OF PLUTO)
NEW HORIZONS SPACECRAFT

"When you get these seats at these tables of power, your obligation is to make sure the conversation is diverse. Because what we saw in this film is that when we pull together men and women, people of every background and color and faith, immigrants who've come here from across the globe to make America their home—when we bring all that brain power to the table, anything is possible, even going to the moon, right?"

—First Lady Michelle Obama, at the White House screening of *Hidden Figures*

CHAPTER THREE
SEPARATE AND
MORE THAN EQUAL
TO THE TASK
NASA'S ROLE IN THE
FIGHT FOR EQUALITY

"You have to look like a girl, act like a lady, think like a man, and work like a dog."
—Macie Roberts, JPL Computers' Supervisor

BEFORE PCS AND MACS, "computers" were human beings. In the late nineteenth and early twentieth centuries, some important number-crunching was being done by women like Williamina Fleming and Annie Jump Cannon, who created systems to analyze and classify stars, systems that laid important foundations for astronomy today. And at the NACA's Langley Memorial Aeronautical Laboratory (LMAL) in the 1930s and '40s, computers were women. These mathematicians performed complicated calculations and equations before the use of calculators, search engines, or any electronic help—all by hand. They played an important role in early aerospace research; some, like Katherine Johnson, played vital roles in major space travel milestones that continue to resonate today.

Katherine Johnson (center) at the Academy Awards

After World War II ended in 1945, Helen Ling left China as a teenager with a full scholarship to the University of Notre Dame and a passion for numbers. Though she majored in art with dreams of designing store windows, she minored in math. She graduated with top grades but had trouble finding work until her brother brought home a COMPUTERS WANTED ad. Her math genius had found a home. She did instrumental work at NASA's Jet Propulsion Laboratory (JPL) on the launch of the Jupiter-C missile, and her computing speed was legendary. "They started with the same equations and were equipped with identical Friden calculators. One of the women would shout, 'Go!' and suddenly the room would fill with the clamor of calculators . . . Soon the whole room was vibrating," author Nathalia Holt writes. "Just when it seemed the room couldn't possibly get any rowdier, Helen would raise her hand and yell, 'Done!' She'd won again." Ling went on to mentor many women at JPL, hiring them as programmers, then encouraging them to get advanced degrees in engineering and guiding them through the JPL system.

In 1935, the NACA hired five women to work as its first computers at Langley. "The women were meticulous and accurate . . . and [NACA] didn't have to pay them very much," says NASA historian Bill Barry. President Roosevelt's Executive Order 8802, the first action by the federal government against employment discrimination in the United States, focused on the defense industry and was, in his words, necessary because "the democratic way of life within the nation can be defended successfully only with the help and support of all groups." That same year, Executive Order 9346 established the Fair Employment Practice Committee and prohibited "discriminatory employment practices by federal agencies and all unions and companies engaged in war-related work."

During World War II, as US men were increasingly drafted into military service, the need for computers grew. The NACA continued to recruit women, who were eager to take positions that offered both entry into aeronautical research and considerably higher salaries than many other fields—though the salaries were still pretty small and the jobs were classified as "subprofessional" despite the women usually having bachelor's degrees. NASA reports that "many former computers noted in interviews that men with similar qualifications were frequently hired as 'junior engineers,' which held a 'professional' classification and had a starting salary of $2,600 per year," while the women's starting salaries as "junior computers" were $1,440 per year. The agency did make a few accommodations that were unusual for that time period, however, such as allowing women to continue working after marriage or having children—something that was often not allowed. A nursery was also added to LMAL facilities in 1943; children could be cared for by nurses on a day-to-day basis, or they could live on the premises for a week at a time.

PROFILE: Janez Lawson

Janez Lawson grew up loving chemistry and math. After graduating from UCLA in 1953 with a degree in chemical engineering, she saw an ad for a job with a description that sounded perfect: "Computers do not need advanced experience or degrees," it read, "but should have an aptitude and interest in mathematics and computing machines." Janez, who was African American, figured that this might be a job open to women in a traditionally white male field. Author Nathalia Holt writes that "for a woman wanting to become an engineer, taking a job as a computer was like entering the field through a secret back door." Lawson aced her interview and impressed NASA so much that she went on to be the first black person hired in a professional position at NASA's Jet Propulsion Lab. She was the only African American woman among her colleagues, and segregated California living also meant that she had to commute for more than an hour each way to work every day, but she persevered and excelled.

THE FIRST LADY ASTRONAUT TRAINEES (FLATS)

While the Mercury 7 have gone down in history as pioneers, there was another group that in many ways trained along with them, though they were not an official NASA program or even a group that met regularly. Nonetheless, this group of women, known as the Mercury 13, and led by pilot Jerrie Cobb, paved the way for women like Sally Ride, Mae Jemison, and Sunita Williams.

Researcher William Randolph Lovelace II, who developed the tests used to assess the Mercury 7, wondered how the same tests would go for women. Though the women's-rights movement was not yet in full swing and the idea of women undergoing rigorous physical training might have been considered pretty wacky at the time, "Lovelace was practical: Women are lighter than men, requiring less fuel to transport them into space," writes journalist Brandon Keim in *Wired* magazine. "They're also less prone to heart attacks, and Lovelace considered them better-suited for the claustrophobic isolation of space." Even before Lovelace, an air force general named Donald Flickinger tried to get a Women in Space Earliest program up and running, but his plans were quickly shelved by the air force. Then Lovelace and Flickinger put their heads together. In 1960, they reached out to decorated pilot Geraldine "Jerrie" Cobb and asked if she'd be willing to undergo the same testing that Lovelace had developed for the Mercury 7. Not only was she willing; she, and most of the women who joined the project, aced it. Thirteen women passed the same tests as the Mercury 7. Their names were Jerrie Cobb, Wally Funk, Irene Leverton, Myrtle "K" Cagle, Jane B. Hart, Gene Nora Stumbough, Jerri Sloan, Rhea Hurrle,

Sarah Gorelick, Bernice "B" Trimble Steadman, Jan Dietrich, Marion Dietrich, and Jean Hixson. These women underwent extensive testing, including X-rays, physical endurance exercises on weighted stationary bicycles, a four-hour eye exam, having ice water shot into their ears to give them vertigo, and a stomach-acid test that required them to swallow a rubber tube. Cobb, Hurrle, and Funk did even more.

"Based on previous experiments in several hundred subjects, it was thought that six hours was the absolute limit of tolerance for this experience before the onset of hallucinations," reports Keim, quoting an article that published the test results. "Cobb, however, spent nine hours and 40 minutes during the experiment, which was terminated by the staff. Subsequently, two other women (Rhea Hurrle and Wally Funk) were also tested, with each spending over 10 hours in the sensory isolation tank before termination by the staff."

Not only that, it seems that their male counterparts took a different, arguably less rigorous path. "During the test, the women were immersed in a lightless tank of cold water. By contrast, John Glenn's memoir recounts being tested in a dimly-lit room, where he was provided with a pen and paper. Glenn's test lasted just three hours."

After Cobb's achievements went public, there was a flurry of interest in the idea of female astronauts—Jerrie Cobb became a bit of a space celebrity. In a press conference, Cobb "told the gathered reporters that she was more afraid of grasshoppers than spaceflight. She even admitted that she was less scared of being alone in space than she was being in a room full of reporters." More women were invited to take part in the research. Pilot, philanthropist, and businesswoman Jacqueline Cochran funded the study and became an adviser to the project. In her fifties, she was older than the average candidate, but she was interested in being an astronaut herself; she urged Lovelace to open his program to a wider range of candidates.

"By the end of the summer of 1961, 19 female pilots had taken astronaut fitness examinations at the Lovelace Clinic. Unlike NASA's male candidates, who competed in group, each woman came to Albuquerque either alone or in pairs for the week of tests. All of the women were skilled airplane pilots with commercial ratings. Most of them were recruited through the Ninety-Nines, a women pilot's organization. Others heard about the testing through friends or newspaper articles and volunteered. The oldest candidate, Jane Hart, was a 41-year-old mother of eight and the wife of a US Senator. The youngest, Wally Funk, was a 23-year-old flight instructor."

The First Lady Astronaut Trainees (FLATs) had more than proven that they were up to the challenges of space travel. NASA remained unconvinced, some even citing menstruation as a possible challenge to putting women in space. NASA also required astronauts to meet educational requirements that were unavailable to women at that time. Lovelace's program was canceled in 1961. Cobb fought hard, petitioning government officials for it to be reinstated. *Popular Science* writer Amy Shira recalls Cobb's 1962 testimony at a congressional hearing called to investigate astronaut qualifications:

"On the first day, Cobb and fellow lady astronaut trainee Janey Hart took the floor. The women were firm. Cobb argued that NASA should work to put a woman in space before the Soviet Union, that she and 12 other exceptionally accomplished female pilots had all passed the same tests as the Mercury astronauts and were ready to fly on a moment's notice. She went on to challenge NASA's requirement that astronauts have jet training. Surely the FLATs, who had more hours in the air than the Mercury astronauts, had equivalent experience. They would be just as successful in spaceflight training as the men had been."

But the women had some surprising opponents. Former benefactor Jacqueline Cochran also testified, saying that the FLAT program should be put on hold while NASA and the country focused on the Moon mission. She had expressed interest in starting her own women-in-space program and reportedly

saw Cobb's efforts as competition. Newly crowned space hero John Glenn added his testimony that the women-in-space program was just too costly for NASA to undertake along with the goal of landing a man on the Moon. The United States had been embarrassed by the Russian head start, and the Apollo mission came first. Glenn also added, "I think this gets back to the way our social order is organized, really. It is just a fact. The men go off and fight the wars and fly the airplanes and come back and help design and build and test them. The fact that women are not in this field is a fact of our social order."

The FLATS, like so many who have sought equal opportunities, were ahead of their time. Russian cosmonaut Valentina Tereshkova became the first woman in space on June 16, 1963. NASA finally accepted women into the astronaut class of 1978. Astronaut Sally Ride became the first American woman in space in 1983. Mae Jemison conducted medical research aboard the space shuttle in 1992, becoming the first black woman in space. Eileen Collins was the first female space shuttle pilot in 1995 and the first to command a space shuttle mission in 1999. Women were taking their rightful place among the stars. But more than 30 years earlier, the FLATS had clearly demonstrated that they were ready.

RACE TO RIGHTS

In 1948, President Truman signed Executive Order 9981 into law, committing to integration of the military, and more black servicemen enlisted in newly desegregated units. In 1957, the Soviet Union launched Sputnik, a feat that reverberated around the world. And a month earlier, President Eisenhower signed in law the Civil Rights Act of 1957, the first federal civil rights legislation since 1875, a demonstration of government support for the cause of racial equality.

At the time, the United States, especially the South, was anything but united—Southern states had entered a period of massive resistance in response to the government's efforts at integration, like *Brown v. Board of Education of Topeka*, which outlawed segregation in public schools. "Racial integration is not going to be accepted in the South," said Virginia Senator Harry Byrd in 1954. White supremacists in the South engaged in violence, voter intimidation,

and discrimination and were often endorsed by local governments.

Meanwhile, as the need grew, the NACA turned to black women to work as computers, segregating their work area; their dining and bathroom facilities were segregated as well. These women, called the West Area Computers, were often given extra tests before they were hired, even when they had college degrees in the subject in question. These were tests that their white counterparts didn't have to take. "Despite having the same education, they had to retake college courses they had already passed and were often never considered for promotions or other jobs within NACA," writes Matt Blitz in *Popular Mechanics.*

Katherine Johnson, whose name became well known after the release of the 2016 book and film *Hidden Figures*, joined the West Area Computers in 1953, analyzing flight-test data and conducting investigations. "I counted everything," Johnson says. "I counted the steps to the road, the steps up to church, the number of dishes and silverware I washed . . . anything that could be counted, I did." Johnson's stellar work should not have been a surprise—she graduated high school at 14 years old, then college at 18, with the highest honors. Johnson went on to do *trajectory analysis* (figuring out the

path that a spacecraft takes under certain conditions, like weather and gravity) for the United States' first human spaceflight: Alan Shepard's Freedom 7 Mission. "The early [Project Mercury] trajectory was a parabola, and it was easy to predict where it would be at any point," Johnson remembered. "When they said they wanted [Shepard's] capsule to come down at a certain place, they were trying to compute when it should start. I said, 'Let me do it. You tell me when you want it and where you want it to land, and I'll do it backward and tell you when to take off.'"

She was moved to the Space Task Force in 1958. In 1960, she coauthored a report with a male engineer. NASA states that "it was the first time a woman in the Flight Research Division had received credit as an author of a research report." Even after electronic computers were in use at NASA, John Glenn insisted that Katherine Johnson double-check the numbers. When it was time for Glenn to make his historic Friendship 7 flight, a worldwide network of electronic computers was established, "linking tracking stations around the world to IBM computers in Washington, DC; Cape Canaveral; and Bermuda." But Glenn and his crew weren't about to put their lives in the hands of machines without reassurance from the best computer they knew—Katherine Johnson.

As a part of the preflight checklist, Glenn asked

engineers to "get the girl"—Katherine Johnson—to run the same numbers through the same equations that had been programmed into the computer, but by hand, on her desktop mechanical calculating machine. "'If she says they're good,'" Katherine Johnson remembers the astronaut saying, "'then I'm ready to go.'"

Former NASA Deputy Administrator Dava Newman points out the significance of Johnson's accomplishments, saying that Johnson "literally wrote the textbook on rocket science" and that her work will provide the foundation for eventual manned Mars missions. "Few Americans have impacted the cause of human exploration so extensively. At NASA, we are proud to stand on Katherine Johnson's shoulders." Newman adds that "Katherine once remarked that while many of her colleagues refrained from asking questions or taking tasks further than merely 'what they were told to do,' she chose instead to ask questions because she wanted to know why."

But the march toward justice continued, and black citizens, from voters to sit-inners, persevered, even as the United States made its way into the Space Age, and launched Alan Shepard into space. It's undeniable that young black scientists, mathematicians, and engineers played a major role in the civil rights and Space Age movements.

PROFILE: DOROTHY VAUGHAN

Dorothy Vaughan, as head of the NACA's West Area Computers unit from 1949 to 1958, was NASA's first African American manager. She was respected as a mathematician, a leader, and an advocate and was often asked to consult on publications and projects. When she and her West Area Computers were moved to desegregated NASA facilities in 1958, Vaughan became a part of the integrated Analysis and Computation Division (ACD), where she worked on the cutting edge of electronic computing. There, Vaughan added to her accomplishments by becoming a FORTRAN programming-language expert and helping other women to do the same. In 1994, Vaughan spoke about the challenges and triumphs of her time at NASA, much of which came during periods of legal and widely accepted discrimination against black people and women. "I changed what I could," she said. "And what I couldn't, I endured." A lifelong educator and changemaker, Dorothy Vaughan died in 2008.

PROFILE: MARY JACKSON

Another of the West Area Computers, Mary Jackson, was a trailblazer in her own right. After graduating from Hampton Institute, doubly degreed in math and physical sciences, she became a math teacher at a local black school. She went on to other jobs, including as a bookkeeper, a receptionist, a homemaker, and an army secretary, until she joined Dorothy Vaughan's crew. Jackson's work drew the attention of engineer Kazimierz Czarnecki, who invited her to work with him on engineering experiments and then suggested that she become an engineer herself.

That wasn't exactly easy for a black woman in segregated Virginia. The graduate-level University of Virginia coursework needed to become an engineer was not available to black women, because it was offered at a segregated school. So Jackson petitioned the city of Hampton to bypass that rule. Her efforts succeeded, and she completed the coursework and became NASA's first black female engineer. "For nearly two decades she enjoyed a productive engineering career, authoring or co-authoring a dozen or so research reports, most [of which] focused on the behavior of the boundary layer of air around airplanes," reports NASA.

Jackson went on to support the inclusion and empowerment of other women at NASA, even leaving engineering and taking a *demotion*—or a move to a lower position—to work in a position where she'd

proud of," says Watson. "We felt that the whole image of black people were riding on us as professionals."

Clyde Foster worked as a technician in the computation lab at Marshall, though he was a qualified professional. Not only that, "You weren't allowed in public facilities," says Foster. "In order to advance, you [had] to satisfy the prerequisites of what the job calls for . . . and they refused to train you." Foster advocated for the development of a training program for black recruits at Alabama A&M, a local black college, so that he and those coming after him could move forward. While he worked at NASA, Foster also established a data-processing laboratory and a computer-science degree program at Alabama A&M, creating more opportunities for black students at NASA. Foster went on to become director of Marshall's Equal Opportunity Office and was later appointed mayor of Triana, Alabama.

To much fanfare in the black press, President Kennedy selected Ed Dwight, who had served as a military pilot and had a degree in aeronautical engineering, as the first black NASA astronaut trainee in 1962. According to *Popular Science*, "With the same qualifications as his space-bound counterparts, Dwight worked as a fully qualified aerospace research pilot but remained the target of racism from both his colleagues and commanding officers."

The plan to send Dwight into space ended with the assassination of President Kennedy on November 22, 1963. In an interview, Dwight maintained that he lost support and Kennedy's successor, Lyndon B. Johnson, replaced him with another black pilot, Robert Henry Lawrence, Jr. Lawrence became part of the air force's Manned Orbital Laboratory Program (MOL), which was a precursor to the Space Shuttle program. Tragically, Lawrence died in a test flight crash before ever making it into space.

NASA historians state that there were some white men within the NASA organization who also advocated for racial equality. One of those was famed rocket scientist Wernher von Braun, who was director of the Marshall Space Flight Center in 1964. He spoke to contractors about civil rights, specifically addressing issues of racial discrimination. He compared policies like poll taxes, which were used to inhibit African American voting, to the situation that divided East and West Germany at the time. "All these regulatory barriers form a 'Berlin Wall' around the ballot box," he said. "I am not going to sit quietly on a major issue like segregation."

PROFILE: GEORGE CARRUTHERS

The camera that Apollo 16 placed on the Moon in 1972 was designed by black astrophysicist George Carruthers. Carruthers graduated from high school during the same year that Sputnik launched. Earning degrees in aeronautical engineering, nuclear engineering, and astronomical engineering, Carruthers went on to work for the Naval Research Laboratory in Washington, DC, where he focused on ultraviolet astronomy. In 1970, his patented "image converter," which detected electromagnetic radiation, recorded the first sighting of molecular hydrogen in outer space. A Carruthers invention captured images of Halley's Comet in 1986, when it passed by Earth for the first time since 1910, and another was used in the Space Shuttle program. Jemison points out that "Carruthers'

President Barack Obama awards the National Medal of Technology and Innovation to Dr. George Carruthers in 2013.

camera was a huge step forward for American science, taking pictures that are the forerunner of today's images from the Hubble Space Telescope. This was one of the most significant scientific achievements by a scientist in the early space program."

It can be lonely at the top. In 1950, Frank Crossley was the first black person to earn a doctorate in metallurgical engineering. "When I have attended national and international meetings in my field . . . I think I have encountered only two African Americans at such meetings over the years." Crossley had experience being the "only"; he was the sole black naval officer trainee in a class of 1,500 in 1945. Crossley went on to work for Lockheed Missiles and Space Company, where he found that despite his skills, racism prevented advancement. His bosses told him, "You are qualified to be a senior member, but because you are so advanced for a Negro, we thought you were content." Crossley went on to receive seven patents for his groundbreaking work.

President Kennedy and Vice President Johnson took important steps to move the country forward on issues of equality. Proposing new civil rights legislation, Kennedy proclaimed that the United States "will not be fully free until all of its citizens are free." After Kennedy's assassination, Johnson addressed Congress, saying, "No memorial oration or eulogy could more eloquently honor President Kennedy's memory than the earliest possible passage of the civil rights bill for which he fought so long." After much opposition from Southern Democrats, Congress passed the Civil Rights Act of 1964, which included the prohibition of racial discrimination in education and employment. On July 2nd of that year, President Lyndon B. Johnson signed it into law.

While legislative change was happening, real-world progress at NASA was occurring, too, but it was slow. Says Steven Moss, "In 1964, according to the New York Times, only eleven [African Americans] were part of the 1,500-member NASA workforce at Cape Canaveral . . . That's only one percent of the NASA workforce in Florida, and even looking throughout the 1960s for the whole agency, NASA was consistently . . . at about three percent."

Decades later, racial and gender integration measures finally began to make their way to the most celebrated NASA contingent: the astronauts. In 1983, Guion "Guy" Bluford Jr. became the first African American in space; Sally Ride, the first woman to fly into space, did so that same year.

FAST FACT On July 25, 2017, the Philadelphia Orchestra premiered "Hold Fast to Dreams," written by composer Nolan Williams Jr. It was a 25-minute piece for an orchestra and choir, commissioned by the Mann Center for the Performing Arts in honor of Guy Bluford Jr.

NASA reports that "by the 1980s, one in ten of the Kennedy Space Center's civil service workforce was made up of minorities, increasing to 17 percent in the mid-1990s." NASA continued to promote inclusion with initiatives like the Science, Engineering, Mathematics and Aerospace Academy, a program for precollegiate minority and female students. NASA reports that "by 2007, minority hiring at Kennedy increased to 23 percent. Today, minorities make up 27.2 percent of just over 2,000 NASA civil service employees at the Florida spaceport."

"Over the past 15 years, women have made up just 15 percent of planetary-mission science teams, even though at least a quarter of planetary scientists are women," writes Paul Voosen in Science magazine. "The disparity is even worse for ethnic minorities: [African Americans] and Hispanics make up 13 percent and 16 percent of the country, respectively, but each group makes up just 1 percent of the nation's planetary scientists." When it comes to inclusion, NASA, like the rest of the country, continues to have a long way to go.

CHAPTER FOUR
LOSING LUSTER

NASA HISTORIANS DESCRIBE President Jimmy Carter as "perhaps the least supportive of US human space efforts of any president in the last half-century." President Carter was trained in engineering, though, and reportedly did get excited about the idea of exploring other planets. Journalist Hugh Sidey wrote in 1978 that President Carter, his "eyes bright with the sense of adventure," listened carefully while being briefed by the late astronomer Carl Sagan about planetary exploration. Carter "urged that any new missions to Mars seek out mountains and valleys and old volcanoes instead of staying on the more level or gently rolling surfaces."

So all was not lost for the space sailors and the rest of their crew. "Our space policy will become more evolutionary rather than centering around a single, massive engineering feat. Pluralistic objectives and needs of our society will set the course for future space efforts," read a presidential statement in 1978.

Still, the following year President Carter considered ending the Space Shuttle program completely. There were a number of technical problems and it was way off schedule. But his advisers believed that they had gone too far to turn back and that the space shuttles were necessary for the launch of military observation satellites that the US used to make sure arms-control agreements were being followed.

On NASA's twentieth anniversary, President Carter honored some of the original space pioneers. Neil Armstrong, Frank Borman, Pete Conrad, John Glenn, Alan Shepard, and Betty Grissom, the wife of astronaut Gus Grissom, were all given the first Congressional Space Medals of Honor. In his speech, the president said, "Like the sea, the land, and the air, space will become an environment in which human beings can live and work for the welfare of their species."

"In the last analysis, the challenge of space takes us very close to the heart of things. It brings us face-to-face with the mysteries of creation, matter, energy, and life. The men we honor today met that challenge and were equal to it. Our nation met that challenge and was equal to it."

—President Jimmy Carter,
Cape Kennedy, October 1, 1978

The Space Shuttle program's first mission, STS-1, was undertaken by Commander John Young and pilot Bob Crippen on the Columbia. It was launched on April 12, 1981, which was the twentieth anniversary of the first human spaceflight in history (Russia's Vostok 1).

The first launch of the space shuttle on April 12, 1981, was huge for NASA—and for the entire country. Even our neighbors in Canada celebrated; Canadian rock band Rush produced a song inspired by the launch of the Columbia called "Countdown." Just after midnight on August 12, 1981, music-video channel MTV debuted with footage of three iconic moments in space history: the Apollo 11 launch, the Moon landing, and Columbia's countdown and lift-off. MTV showed an astronaut on the moon, saluting the MTV flag. "Ladies and gentlemen: Rock and roll," announced a voice-over.

The space shuttle era had begun.

On its first mission, Columbia orbited the Earth 37 times. Shuttles were a new breed of spacecraft designed to "launch like a rocket and land like a plane." Columbia was built to be used over and over again. Columbia's STS-2 mission was the first time a space vehicle was reused. Columbia went on a total of 28 missions, including: 1983's STS-9, which carried Ulf Merbold, the first West German citizen to enter space; STS-61-C in 1986, which carried Franklin Chang Díaz, known as the first Hispanic American in space, as well as Representative Bill Nelson of Florida, the first member of the House of Representatives to enter space; and STS-93, launched in 1999, which was led by the first female shuttle commander, Eileen Collins, and

Kendrik Lamar with MTV's now-iconic Moonman award

which also carried the Chandra X-ray space observatory, named for Indian-American Nobel Prize–winning astrophysicist Subrahmanyan Chandrasekhar. Columbia carried Spacelab 1, the space laboratory built by the European Space Agency that was the precursor to the International Space Station (ISS). Spacelab 1 carried more than 70 experiments in several scientific fields, including astronomy, solar physics, life sciences, and materials science. The Columbia also carried the astronauts and tools that successfully repaired the Hubble Space Telescope in 2002.

The Space Shuttle program made history in many ways.

FAST FACT Space shuttle Challenger was the first orbiter to come home for landing, touching back down on Kennedy's Shuttle Landing Facility on February 11, 1984, to conclude the STS-41B mission. Two astronauts, Robert L. Stewart and Bruce McCandless II, took NASA's first untethered spacewalks on that mission.

WHAT IS MISSION CONTROL, AND WHAT'S REALLY ON ALL OF THOSE SCREENS?

We see it depicted in television and movies—rooms full of people and computer monitors, lights flashing, beeps beeping, countdowns in progress. NASA's Mission Control Centers (MCCs) remotely operate spacecraft from different locations around the world. NASA instructor and engineer Robert Frost explained to *The Verge* what goes on at the MCC in Houston that helps to operates the ISS:

> "In any given month, somewhere around 50,000 commands are sent to the ISS—including things like orbit correction maneuvers to keep the vehicle in a stable position around Earth or to put the station out of harm's way from space debris."

The Atlantic reports that "mission control . . . monitors all the onboard systems—electrical, life support, [information technology], communications. A vast team on the ground supports the station—more than 1,000 people for every astronaut in orbit.

And while astronauts get to kick off the workday, the pace and rhythm of the day are unequivocally set by the people on the ground. Life on the station is managed via spreadsheet: Every minute of each astronaut's workday is mapped out in blocks devoted to specific tasks. When an astronaut clicks on a time block, it expands to present all the steps necessary to perform the task at hand—whether it's conducting an hours-long experiment on the behavior of fire in zero-G or stowing supplies from a cargo ship."

Teams of people, usually about 50, work at desks called *consoles* that are packed with computer monitors, just like we see on TV or in films. "Each of those people are a certified flight controller for a particular discipline (e.g., electrical power, thermal control, trajectory, planning, etc.)," writes Frost. "They trained for one to three years (depending on the complexity of the discipline) and were thoroughly evaluated in simulations before they were allowed to sit in this room." The flight controllers are managed by a flight

director, who is the big boss. "The flight director is the person ultimately responsible for the vehicle," explains Frost.

One of the computers on each person's console is for their regular day-to-day work—creating timelines, going over procedures, etc.—and the rest connect to the spacecraft that they're controlling. "We have, basically, computer systems and lots of screens filled with data," said Flight Director Mary Lawrence on NASA's *Houston We Have a Podcast*. "That data's coming from the computer network [that's] essentially on the space craft." There are also large screens in the front of the MCC that show the vehicle's location, any warnings, clocks that count down to specific events, and more.

On the ISS, Mission Control's main job is to support the onboard crew as they conduct their science experiments and research. So basically, Mission Control is controlling the vehicle. "We do a lot of the day-to-day flying of the space station to make sure that the crew can do what only astronauts can do," explained Lawrence, "which is science in space."

The team members wear headsets to use for all official mission communication. And that communication is vital at all times. "It's 100 percent the flight controllers on the ground flying the space station," said NASA Flight Director Zebulon Scoville in an interview on *The Verge*. "If that capability is lost, then that can be a risk to the mission."

Each person has a dedicated "voice loop," which is kind of like their direct extension, specific to them. Then there are loops that everyone has access to, for information that everyone on the team needs to hear. "There's a loop to talk to the flight director, and everyone is listening . . . So I generally talk to every-

one on the flight loop so that everyone can hear the conversations that we're having and the decisions that are being made," said Lawrence. "But if I want to talk to someone and not everyone else needs to hear it, I can call on certain other loops. So I can talk to our international partners, for example. I can coordinate with the European flight director or the Japanese flight director or the Russian flight director on other coordination loops as well." There is a person called a "CapCom" who is the one person who communicates directly with the crew on the spacecraft.

Like any job at NASA, it takes a lot of training to become a member of a Mission Control team. "Most people that come in have an engineering background," said Lawrence, who has a degree in mechanical engineering. "I'd say that's the most common degree, but a space science–related background is also common. So you come in already with kind of an engineering way of thinking . . . And then, you're taken, within your team, to really start learning specifics about the system. So you spend a fair amount of time just learning how the system works. Once you get deep enough into your training flow, you start into what we call simulations, where you practice doing mission operations . . . And once you pass your final evaluation, you spend some amount of time on console, probably with a mentor or someone sitting next to you that's been doing the job, and they're evaluating how you perform in real time. And that takes probably about a year and a half to make it into." Lawrence adds that communication and collaboration skills are key to being a good MCC team member. And there's one more thing that helps them do their job . . . "Coffee is essential," she added.

TRAGEDY IN THE SKIES

CHALLENGER

Challenger had many causes to celebrate. It was NASA's second shuttle to reach space. Its premier mission included the first spacewalk of NASA's Space

Shuttle program, conducted by Story Musgrave and Donald Peterson. Challenger carried the first female astronaut, Sally Ride, on STS-7 in 1983, and the first

African American astronaut, Guion Bluford, on STS-8 that same year.

On its tenth flight, mission STS-51-L, Challenger carried physicist and mission specialist Ronald L. Mc-Nair, the second African American in space, who planned to record a saxophone solo onboard; Ellison Onizuka, the first Hawaiian, Asian American and Japanese American in space; and Sharon Christa McAuliffe, a high school social studies teacher who completed NASA's Teacher in Space training program with the goal of being the first civilian in space. Other crew members were Commander Francis R. Scobee, pilot Michael J. Smith, Judith Resnick, and Gregory Jarvis. The world watched as, 73 seconds into its flight, Challenger broke apart, killing all onboard. It was found that it had been launched in conditions that were too cold, which contributed to technical failures.

After the Challenger tragedy, NASA's plans to send civilians into space were put on hold for 22 years.

There is a monument to the Challenger crew at Arlington National Cemetery in Virginia. Numerous schools have been named after the crew members, and the film *Star Trek IV: The Voyage Home* was dedicated to them. On April 5, 1986, musician Jean Michel Jarre played "Last Rendez-Vous" in tribute to his friend Ronald McNair. The original plan had been for McNair to join in on saxophone, in what would have been the first music recording from space.

McAuliffe was selected from more than 11,400 applicants to become the first private citizen in space. As part of the Teacher in Space program, created in 1984 by the Reagan administration, the New Hampshire high school social studies teacher planned to film science lessons that would be shared with students around the world. "I cannot join the space program and restart my life as an astronaut, but this opportunity to connect my abilities as an educator with my interests in history and space is a unique opportunity to fulfill my early fantasies," she wrote in her application to the program. McAuliffe also hoped to inspire more people to enter the teaching profession.

In 2018, NASA announced that astronauts Joe Acaba and Ricky Arnold, both former teachers, would do some of McAuliffe's planned lessons on the ISS as a tribute to her and her work. The Challenger Center, an organization started by families of the victims of the tragedy, is working with NASA to carry out this plan. "For more than 30 years, we have continued the mission of the Challenger crew, reaching more than five million students with our hands-on STEM

[science, technology, engineering, and mathematics] programs," said Challenger President and CEO Lance Bush in a statement. "We are honored to have the opportunity to complete Christa's lessons and share them with students and teachers around the world."

COLUMBIA

It was Columbia's twenty-eighth mission: STS-107. Launched on January 16, 2003, it was a large research mission, and some of the studies included looking at why spaceflight changes human bones, why astronauts get more dehydrated in space, and other effects of space travel on the body. The crew also conducted experiments for the European Space Agency, including the effects of microgravity on fire and the behavior of bacteria and antibiotics in space. The crew included Kalpana Chawla, the first Indian woman in space; Ilan Ramon; Commander Rick D. Husband; pilot William McCool; Michael P. Anderson; David M. Brown; and Laurel Blair Salton Clark. On February 1, 2003, the Columbia exploded upon re-entry into the Earth's atmosphere. All of the crew died instantly. It was discovered later that a hole in the spacecraft's wing caused the accident. "The Shuttle was getting old, and it wasn't as safe as we thought," says NASA historian Bill Barry.

In 2004, NASA's Mars Exploration Rover (MER) Spirit landed on Mars, holding a plaque with the names of the seven Columbia astronauts on it. The MER landing area is officially named the Columbia Memorial Station in their honor. Seven asteroids were named after the crew members. Roundworms onboard Columbia for research survived the disaster, and some of their descendants were launched on the shuttle Endeavor in 2011. "The Columbia crew's actual mission was an outstanding success . . . The science of the STS-107 mission was used. The International Space Station currently enjoys a waste-water recycling system that was first tested in space by the 107 Columbia crew. Cancer research was advanced. Knowledge of human adaptability to microgravity was increased," points out writer Chris Gebhardt. The work of the Columbia crew lives on.

PROFILE: Ilan Ramon

Air Force Colonel Ilan Ramon made history as Israel's first astronaut. Selected in 1997 as part of a special agreement between NASA and the Israeli Space Agency, the former fighter pilot moved to the US with his family and trained as an astronaut for 4 ½ years. Part of his work on the Columbia mission involved observations of dust storms to study global climate changes and conducting an experiment planned by Ort Kiryat Motzkin Middle School students in Israel. This "chemical garden" study compared the growth of crystals in space and on Earth.

Ramon, the son of a Holocaust survivor, hoped to be a symbol of peace and cooperation as a member of the Columbia crew. In an interview on Space.com, Ramon said, "There is no better place to emphasize the unity of people in the world than flying in space. We are all the same people, we are all human beings, and I believe that most of us—almost all of us—are good people."

After the 2003 Columbia disaster, the Space Shuttle program was phased out. President Bush made the announcement: "The shuttle's chief purpose over the next several years will be to help finish assembly of the International Space Station . . . The space shuttle, after nearly 30 years of duty, will be retired from service." The final shuttle mission was Atlantis, with a purpose of delivering equipment to the ISS. It launched on July 8, 2011, and landed 13 days later.

"We'll continue our quest in space. There will be more shuttle flights and more shuttle crews, and, yes, more volunteers, more civilians, more teachers in space. Nothing ends here."

—President Ronald Reagan, January 1986

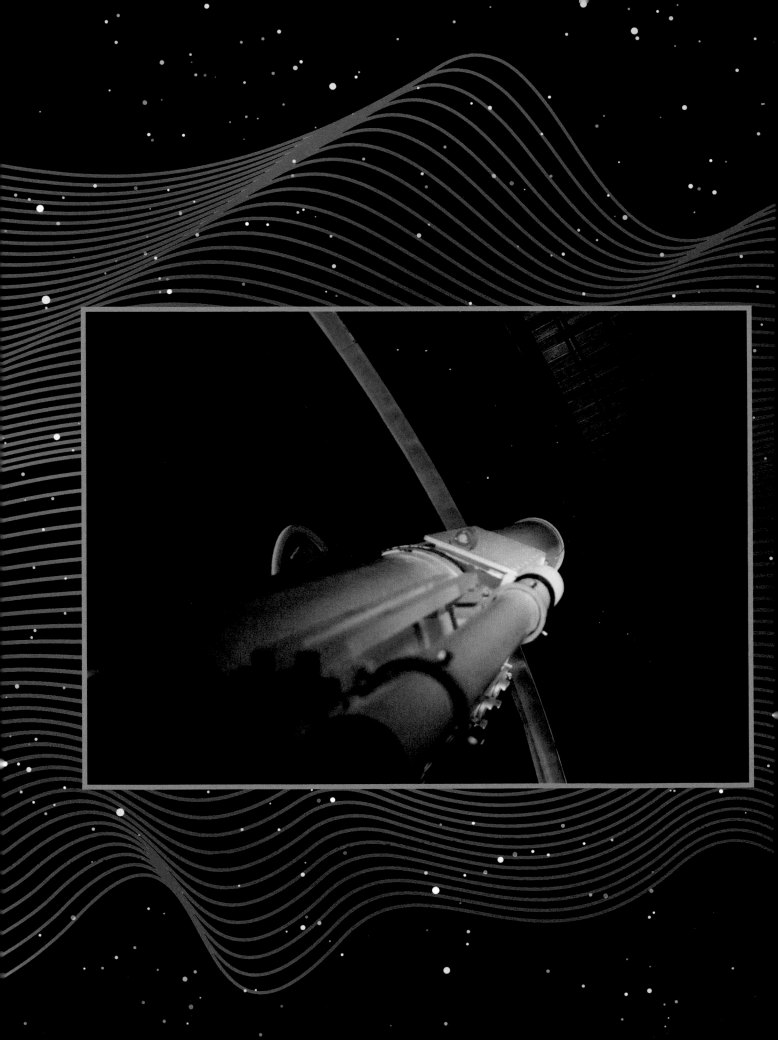

CHAPTER FIVE

"STAR WARS" AND SEEING STARS

Space shuttles carrying humans were grounded until the Discovery's return to flight mission in 1988. On the second day of the mission, the crew was awakened with a call from actor and comedian Robin Williams, saying, "Gooooooooooood morning, Discovery!"

ON MARCH 23, 1983, President Ronald Reagan made a big announcement about the development of a new nuclear-defense system, one that would make nuclear weapons "impotent and obsolete." He called it the Strategic Defense Initiative (SDI), but because it involved space lasers that would blast Soviet missiles out of the sky, many jokingly called it "Star Wars." After many dollars and no success, and with the arrival of the Cold War's end in 1991, the initiative was officially renamed and refocused in 1993 by the Clinton administration.

Reagan's announcement the following year, on January 25, 1984, was more successful: NASA's next big challenge was to develop an international space station. "A space station will permit quantum leaps in our research in science, communications, and in metals and lifesaving medicines [that] could be manufactured only in space," Reagan said in his State of the

Union Address. "We want our friends to help us meet these challenges and share in their benefits. NASA will invite other countries to participate so we can strengthen peace, build prosperity, and expand freedom for all who share our goals." A space station was something NASA had been wanting to do for a long time, and now not only was the president offering strong support; Reagan had issued an invitation to US allies around the world to get in on the space station research game. Global cooperation was to be a central part of the endeavor.

The '80s also saw a growing interest in the possibility of profit from space activity. NASA's Office of Commercial Programs was created and got busy looking at ways to get the private sector involved in space. Businesses wanted to figure out how to make money from space exploration, and the government wanted NASA to look at commercial uses for its technology.

MAKING CONTACT WITH BILLIONS: CARL SAGAN

"He led a feverish existence, with multiple careers tumbling over one another, as if he knew he wouldn't live to an old age. Among other things, he served as an astronomy professor at Cornell, wrote more than a dozen books, worked on NASA robotic missions, edited the scientific journal *Icarus* and somehow found time to park himself, repeatedly—arguably compulsively—in front of TV cameras. He was the house astronomer, basically, on Johnny Carson's *Tonight Show*. Then, in an astonishing burst of energy in his mid-'40s, he co-created and hosted a 13-part PBS television series, *Cosmos*."

—Joel Achenbach, *Smithsonian*

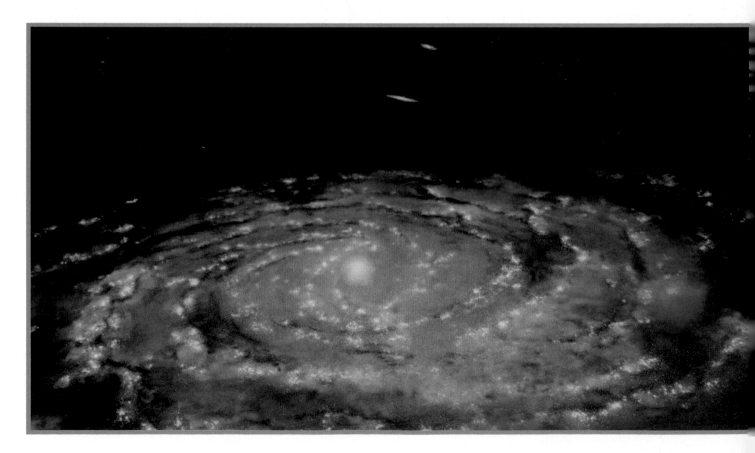

Not many people could remind us of how inconsequential and small we are as eloquently as Carl Sagan. His impact on the field of astronomy, on popular culture's fascination with space, and on our search for life on other planets is vast. Sagan testified before Congress about UFOs, wrote a science-fiction novel called *Contact*, and was an antinuclear activist. He worked with NASA on many occasions, including for the Mariner 2, Viking, Pioneer, Voyager, and Galileo missions. In the '70s, he was one of the first to predict that it was a *greenhouse effect* (or warming of a planet's atmosphere) that made Venus's atmosphere so lead-meltingly hot, and he warned of the impact of climate change in his 1980 book, *Cosmos*.

From a very young age, Sagan was interested in the wonders and mysteries of space. Born in Brooklyn, New York, he once wrote, "My parents were not scientists. They knew almost nothing about science. But in introducing me simultaneously to skepticism and to wonder, they taught me the two uneasily cohabiting modes of thought that are central to the scientific method." A visit to the 1939 New York World's Fair sparked an interest in science and technology, and Sagan took a solo trip to the library to check out books about stars when he was only five years old. Trips to the Hayden Planetarium at the American Museum of Natural History burned the flame even brighter.

Sagan went on to earn degrees in physics, astronomy, and astrophysics, and he became director of Cornell University's Laboratory for Planetary Studies in 1968. "He worked very hard for his students, got

them jobs, worried about their education," said Sagan biographer William Poundstone in an interview. Pulitzer Prize–winning Sagan was a master science communicator; *Cosmos* spent over a year as a best-selling book, and the PBS television version reached more than half a billion people around the world in 1980. Sagan also worked with NASA on pioneering research in the fields of *exobiology*, or the study of extraterrestrial life, and *astrobiology*, the study of the origin and evolution of life in the universe.

When 17-year-old Neil DeGrasse Tyson was deciding where to attend college in 1975, he received a surprise invitation to visit Cornell from Sagan. In an interview on PBS, Tyson—who went on to host the rebooted *Cosmos* show and became director of the Hayden Planetarium—recalled how Sagan took him on a personal tour of the campus, gifted Tyson a signed copy of one of his books, and gave Tyson his home phone number. Tyson said, "To this day, I have this duty to respond to students, who are inquiring about the universe as a career path . . . the way Carl Sagan responded to me."

As George H. W. Bush took office and the '80s came to a close, many in government were seeking a new challenge for NASA and the space program that would restore confidence in and build enthusiasm for the agency's work. On the twentieth anniversary of the Apollo 11 landing, President Bush announced what became known as the Space Exploration Initiative. "First, for the coming decade, for the 1990s: Space Station Freedom, our critical next step in all our space endeavors. And next, for the new century: back to the Moon; back to the future. And this time, back to stay. And then a journey into tomorrow, a journey to another planet: a manned mission to Mars." Added Bush: "History proves that we have never lost by pressing the limits of our frontiers." Unfortunately, many believed that the country had reached the limit when it came to NASA. President Bush was unable to get congressional and public support for the initiative, and it withered away. In 1990, a White House commission concluded that "NASA is currently overcommitted in terms of program obligations relative to resources available—in short, it is trying to do too much."

NASA scientists' main focus was a little closer to home, anyway. After the Challenger tragedy, astronaut Sally Ride led a NASA task force that prioritized a research program called Mission to Planet Earth (MTPE). MTPE's goal was to "study and characterize [from space] our home planet on a global scale . . . Mission to Planet Earth is not the sort of major program the public normally associates with an agency famous for Apollo, Viking, and Voyager. But this initiative is a great one, not because it offers tremendous excitement and adventure, but because of its fundamental importance to humanity's future on this planet."

TELESCOPES: EXPANDING OUR VISION

Why can't we just use a ginormous telescope on Earth to see objects in outer space? Why is a space telescope such a great idea? Why did we need the Hubble Space Telescope in the first place?

Well, for one thing, there's a space issue. And a cost issue. But the real reason is: us. Or more accurately, our atmosphere. "The big advantage of a space telescope," says NASA's Lee Feinberg, "is that you are not looking through the blurry atmosphere of the Earth, and that means you can get much clearer pictures of objects that are farther away and further back in time." When we look through a telescope on Earth, the light we see is passing through the Earth's atmosphere—and all the gunk it contains. Even when the skies seem clear to us, there are gazillions of molecules in our air that scatter the light.

(That's why stars seem to "twinkle.") Our atmosphere also helps to block light that's dangerous to humans, like ultraviolet rays and X-rays. This is good for our health but not so good for space vision. So in order to see clearly and find, as US astronomer Edwin P. Hubble said, "something we had not expected," we needed to put a telescope in space.

HUBBLE TROUBLE

Americans had been dreaming of a space telescope for decades. German rocket scientist Hermann Oberth was thinking about it in the 1920s, and astrophysicist Lyman Spitzer proposed a plan for one in 1946. And he kept on proposing and advocating for close to 30 years. His perseverance paid off—Spitzer had the pleasure of working with the Hubble Telescope after its launch. "I have a weakness of character," Spitzer once said, "a fascination with the spectacular. But then I have a sort of theory of our weaknesses being our strengths."

The Hubble was named for Edwin P. Hubble, whose research confirmed the theory of the "raisin bread dough" expanding universe. Hubble created a commonly used galaxy classification system and was

> **RAISIN BREAD DOUGH ANALOGY:**
> To aid in explaining the expansion of the universe, imagine it's a loaf of raisin bread dough. The dough will expand and rise, and as it does, the raisins will separate farther from each other. They move far apart but will remain in the dough.

also instrumental in the development of the Hale 200-inch telescope, which was the largest on Earth for many years. The Hubble became the first-ever optical telescope in the world to be housed in and work from space when it was launched on April 24, 1990.

Everything promised that the future—and our view of outer space—would be bright!

Hubble Telescope under construction

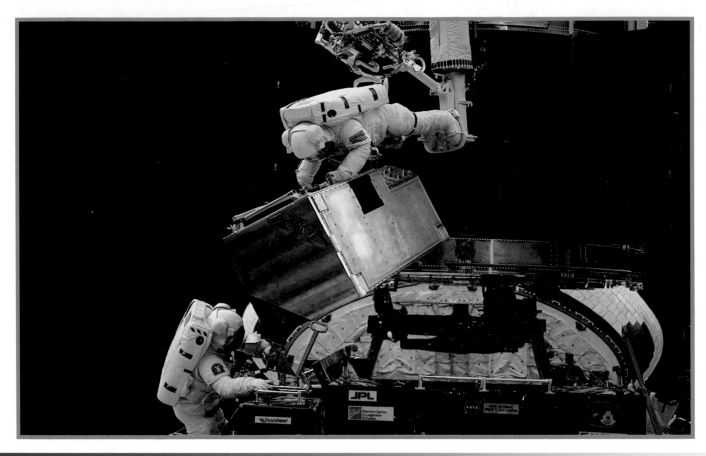

EYEGLASSES IN SPACE

Well, not exactly. At least, not at first. After the much-heralded launch of the Hubble, the view through the telescope was positively blurry. Deemed Hubble Trouble, it turned out that there was a flaw in one of the Hubble's mirrors, and on December 2, 1993, seven astronauts on the space shuttle Endeavor went up to fix it—kind of like space opticians. "The astronauts were putting these instruments in that were really like contact lenses that would fix the blurriness problem," says Feinberg. Over a period of five days, teams of two spacewalked back and forth, making the repairs.

> "Hubble made a major leap forward in really showing the magnitude of the universe. I mean, there are at least 100 billion galaxies, and each galaxy has hundreds of billions of stars. And the farthest galaxy that Hubble has detected is over 13 billion light-years away. It's absolutely amazing."
>
> —Charles Elachi, former director of NASA's Jet Propulsion Laboratory

"This was the most complex shuttle mission that had ever been undertaken," said team member Jeffrey Hoffman at a symposium marking the twentieth anniversary of the repair mission.

The mission was a huge success—our "window on the universe" was spectacularly clear! NASA had once again realized the impossible: an observatory in space. With the Hubble, we could see beyond our wildest dreams. We could see the births and deaths of distant stars and galaxies colliding. Once again, NASA had helped us see new possibilities.

PROFILE: EDWIN HUBBLE

"I knew that even if I were second or third rate, it was astronomy that mattered."

—Edwin Hubble, astronomer

By the sound of this, Edwin Hubble was a pretty humble guy, even though his work launched what British astrophysicist and bestselling author of *A Brief History of Time* Stephen Hawking called "one of the great intellectual revolutions of the twentieth century." But, in addition to being a brilliant scientist, Hubble was an athlete, a decorated soldier, and possibly even a bit of a party dude by some accounts. Apparently he was also proud enough of his work to "campaign" for a Nobel Prize in Physics in the 1940s; some say that he even hired a publicist to help garner support. But astronomy was not considered eligible for a

Nobel Prize at that point, and Hubble died without the prestigious award (many believe he was on the verge of getting it at the time of his death). However, his legacy lives on: There's an asteroid named after him, and observations made by the Hubble Telescope were an important part of the 2011 Nobel Prize in Physics winners' work. And let's not forget that the telescope and Hubble's Law were named after him. One of the Hubble's goals was to help figure out the expansion rate of the universe, and it was because of Edwin Hubble that we realized the universe was expanding in the first place!

KENNEDY SPACE CENTER
1990

PROFILE: HENRIETTA LEAVITT

Born in 1868, Henrietta Leavitt was an astronomer whose work was instrumental to the development of Edwin Hubble's theory of an expanding universe. Working as a "human computer" for Edward C. Pickering at the Harvard Observatory, Leavitt discovered that there was a relationship between a star's brightness and its *absolute magnitude*, or how bright it appears at the standard distance from Earth of 32.6 light-years. According to the website *A Mighty Girl*,

"She spent years measuring star positions and sizes and, over time, discovered that certain stars had a fixed pattern to their changes—a discovery that allowed astronomers to understand the true size of the universe . . . [This] brought Leavitt recognition as a pioneer of astronomical science." The asteroid 5383 Leavitt and the Leavitt Moon crater are named after her. They also honor deaf astronomers, because Leavitt grew ill after college and became deaf.

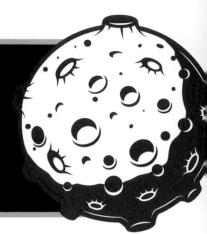

HOW TELESCOPES WORK

Why is it hard to see something as it gets farther away from us? Is there a way for us to develop superhero-style vision? Or at least superhero eyeglasses?

Telescopes are a little like superhero glasses. They have developed into powerful tools that literally help us see through time, but the basic principles that make them work were discovered centuries ago.

Hans Lippershey, a Dutch eyeglass maker, was the first to apply for a patent for his magnifying device that he named a *kijker*, or "looker." He said that it was an instrument "for seeing things far away as if they were nearby." There are a few different stories of how he came up with the idea; one legend has it that he saw children playing with curved eyeglass lenses, looking through two lenses to make a weather vane seem closer than it was. This design using curved glass is called *refracting*—it bends light to help create the image.

Galileo Galilei is famous for being connected with the development of the telescope—and for his rather poetic name. While he is not (as is often believed) the inventor of the telescope, he did work to modify and increase the power of Lippershey's designs. Only then did he become the first known person to use the instrument to look up and out into space and publish a record of what he saw. The first

thing he saw? The Moon. Up until then, people had imagined the Moon to be smooth—that's what it looked like from Earth. But Galileo's study of the Moon led to the discovery that the Moon was "not smooth, even and perfectly spherical . . . but, on the contrary, [it is] uneven, rough, and crowded with depressions and bulges. And it is like the face of the Earth itself, which is marked here and there with chains of mountains and depths of valleys." He went on to publish his findings of what his telescope and a little handy math led him to learn about on the Moon, Jupiter, and the Milky Way in a book called *Sidereus Nuncius*, or *The Starry Messenger*, in 1610—and what a mind-blowing message it sent. Saturn had rings! The Milky Way wasn't a patch of clouds but was made up of stars! The heavens weren't "perfect," as had been previously thought—but they sure were mysterious and magnificent.

FUN FACT Galileo's telescope is on view at the Museo Galileo in Italy. But if you amateur astronomers can't make it there, you *can* build a replica from his instructions. He took great notes.

In 1668, Isaac Newton, who kept busy doing things like discovering gravity, understanding white light, and creating calculus, also made a little extra time to refine the reflecting telescope, which improved on Lippershey's earlier refracting design in many ways. What made it better?

Think of your eye as a screen—if an object is very far away, it seems smaller, and it can't take up enough

room on your screen to be visible. Your eye needs to be able to collect enough light from an object to create and magnify an image of it. In order to see a distant object, we'd need ginormous eyes. A refracting telescope bends the light and magnifies the image; Galileo's telescope used a lens to collect light from the images he observed in space. But when light passes through lenses, the different colors pass at dif-

ferent angles and don't quite come to one focal point, causing *chromatic aberration*. Aka, the larger the lens is, the more distorted the image becomes, getting bigger and blurrier. Newton decided to use a mirror instead, bouncing light from a surface. Because it didn't go through a lens, the distortion problem was solved. Others had thought of this before (Italian monk Niccolo Zucchi, for instance, whose book on optics inspired Newton), but Newton's invention was the one that worked. Both refracting and reflecting telescopes are still used today.

If you're in the market for one: A refractor version works well for observing larger and closer objects, like the Moon. If you want to see farther out, then a reflector version makes more sense. (Want both? There are telescopes that combine both mirrors and lenses, called catadioptric telescopes.)

Most commonly used refracting telescopes work with a two-lens principle: a big lens (the *objective lens*) collects lots of light and focuses it to a smaller point inside of the telescope (called the *focal point*); then a second, smaller lens (called the *eyepiece lens*) takes all of that light and works like a magnifying glass to make the image look larger.

WAIT A MINUTE . . . IS A TELESCOPE LIKE A TIME MACHINE? WHEN WE LOOK THROUGH A TELESCOPE, ARE WE ACTUALLY LOOKING BACK IN TIME?

Rich Chomko, New Jersey public school teacher and physical-sciences educator at the American Museum of Natural History, says: "Absolutely! The farther we look in distance, the further 'back in time' we are looking." So for instance, "at 8 ¹/₂ *light-minutes* away [or the distance traveled in 8 ¹/₂ minutes by light moving at light speed], when you see the Sun, it's not as it is at that moment but as it was 8 ¹/₂ minutes ago. If it exploded, we wouldn't know until 8 ¹/₂ minutes later."

WHOA! BUT WAIT, THERE'S MORE . . .

Chomko continues, "Astronomers can use this 'time traveling' in many ways—most importantly to test their theories of stellar and galactic evolution. Instead of having to wait geologic amounts of time to test theories, they can just look for evidence at varying distances for different star or galactic types. Of course, for the farthest distances you need more and more powerful telescopes. But depending on what you are studying, it might not be as difficult as you might think."

So telescopes are basically magic. Science is so cool.

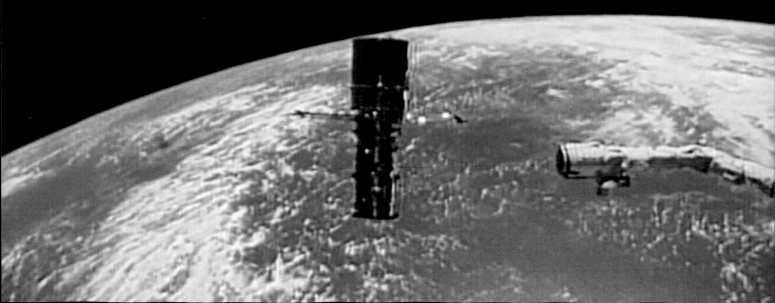

SPIRAL GALAXY M100
50 MILLION LIGHT-YEARS AWAY

CHAPTER SIX
WORLD PEACE...
IN SPACE

THE '90S, BEGINNING WITH the Hubble trouble, continued the challenging times for NASA. Its budget was decreased, even while other government agencies' budgets were significantly increased. It was more and more difficult for NASA to conduct its work. The Clinton administration announced an official "end to the *Star Wars* era" (but never fear: the movies continued). Advisers told President Clinton to cancel the space station program, but then NASA worked with its Russian counterparts to propose another way: redesigning the existing space station Freedom with US and Russian parts. NASA believed it would be cheaper and more efficient, and the Clinton administration saw new possibilities for a positive relationship with Russia. A new deal was done, and the dream of an international space station would live

to see another day. "This is a promising moment," said President Clinton. "Instead of building weapons in space, Russian scientists will help us build the International Space Station."

In the mid-'90s, NASA scientists made an exciting announcement: They had found what could be traces of live bacteria in a meteorite, discovered in Antarctica, that had originated on Mars. It wasn't little green men, but still—possibility of life on Mars! President Clinton held a press conference, saying, "I am determined that the American space program will put its full intellectual power and technological prowess behind the search for further evidence of life on Mars." But . . . the enthusiasm fizzled out. A big meeting was held to discuss the future of NASA's programming and budget, and that was pretty much it.

> "It was the creativity that drew me to it. The possibilities. Understanding what was going on in the world around me."

—Mae Jemison, first African American woman in space

PROFILE: mae jemison

When Mae Jemison was in kindergarten, her teacher asked the class what they'd like to be when they grew up. "And I said, 'I want to be a scientist,'" Jemison remembered in a profile from the National Library of Medicine. "And [the teacher] looked at me and she said, 'Don't you mean a nurse?'"

But from a young age, Mae Jemison "was excited about the world" [around her].

"The issue back *then* was . . . that's the only thing [my teacher] could see a little girl growing up to do that had something to do with sciences. So she was trying to help guide me and counsel me . . . as to what was possible. But I really just put my hands on my hips, and I said, 'No, I mean a scientist.'"

Jemison was born in Decatur, Alabama, in 1956 and fell in love with science early. She grew up enjoying the outdoors and the natural world and had an uncle who talked to her about the stars, the Sun, and even Einstein's theory of relativity when she was as young as six. She explored anthropology, archaeology, and astronomy. "I always assumed that I was supposed to be able to understand these things. It wasn't something that was outside of the ordinary for me." Growing up in the early days of NASA's space exploration, "I followed the Gemini, the Mercury, and the Apollo Programs; I had books about them, and I always assumed I would go into space. Not necessarily as an astronaut; *I* thought because we were on the Moon when I was 11 or 12 years old, that we would be going to Mars—I'd be going to work on Mars as a scientist." As a child, she noticed that NASA seemed to send only white men into space. "There were no women, and it was all white males—and, in fact, I thought that was one of the dumbest things in the world, because I used to always worry, believe it or not as a little girl, I was like, 'What would aliens think

of humans?' You know, 'These are the only humans?'"

Jemison went on to college at 16 years old, graduating with degrees in engineering and Afro-American studies. She went on to medical school and then practiced medicine as a refugee-camp volunteer in Asia and as a Peace Corps medical officer in West Africa. A doctor advised her that a medical degree might be a boost to her engineering research. "You can't just build this little piece of equipment and then not figure out whether it's going to be useful to a person," she says. "Will the person actually use it? How is it going to change their lifestyle? Being in medicine was going to be very important, so that's how I ended up going to medical school." After she returned to the US, she was selected by NASA for astronaut training in 1987, and the rest is history. As the first African American woman in space, Jemison conducted bone-cell research as a mission specialist on the space shuttle Endeavor in 1992—a joint mission between NASA and the Japanese space agency. Astronauts often bring special personal possessions along for the ride when they take their space journeys; for her 190 hours, 30 minutes, and 23 seconds in space, Jemison brought a few meaningful items:

"When I went into space, I carried a number of things up with me," said Jemison in a Ted talk. "I carried a poster by Alvin Ailey . . . of Judith Jamison performing the dance "Cry," dedicated to all black women everywhere. [I carried] a Bundu statue, which was from the Women's Society in Sierra Leone, and a certificate for the Chicago Public School students to work to improve their science and math. Folks asked me, 'Why did you take up what you took up?' and I had to say, 'Because it represents human creativity, the creativity that allowed us—that we were required to have—to conceive and build and launch the space shuttle, [which] springs from the same source as the imagination and analysis it took to carve a Bundu statue, or the ingenuity it took to design, choreograph, and stage 'Cry.' Each one of them [is a] different manifestation, incarnation, of creativity—avatars of human creativity. And that's what we have to reconcile in our minds, how these things fit together."

It's been reported that Jemison is afraid of heights, which might be a little hard to overcome as an astronaut. But she has said that "she relied on the strength of her ego to push forward."

In addition to a lifelong love of dance (she considered a performing arts career before she became a doctor and scientist, but her mom said, "You can always dance if you're a doctor, but you can't doctor if you're a dancer"), Jemison spends time studying languages. She speaks fluent Russian, Swahili, and Japanese. She also skis and sews, and she loves photography and collecting African art. After her time at NASA, Jemison founded the Jemison Group, which looks at ways to apply technology to daily life around the world. "As a Peace Corps area medical officer, I learned a lot about developing countries, about health care in those situations," she says. "And as an astronaut, I learned an awful lot about remote-sensing satellite telecommunications and all of these nice things . . . and so I could put them together. And that really set the tone for a lot of the work that I did later on, which was looking at how . . . you use advanced technologies in developing countries. How . . . you blend social issues with technology design."

Jemison and her work inspired the Mae C. Jemison Science and Space Museum at Wright Junior College in Chicago and the Mae C. Jemison Academy, a Chicago public school. She went on to do many other activities, including founding The Earth We Share, an international science camp for young people that encourages science literacy for everyone. "Science literacy is not about people becoming professional scientists, but rather [about people] being able to read an article in the newspaper about health [and] the environment and figure out how to vote responsibly on it," she says. Jemison believes in the value of both science and arts education. "Science provides an understanding of a universal experience, and arts provides a universal understanding of a personal experience. That's what we have to think about—that they're all part of a continuum . . . it would be really foolish to choose either one, right? Intuitive versus analytical? That's a foolish choice. It's foolish, just like trying to choose between being realistic or idealistic. You need both in life."

FUN FACT Jemison, a longtime *Star Trek* fan, was very inspired by Nichelle Nichols's portrayal of communications officer Lieutenant Uhura on the television show. When she was on the space shuttle, she would start her shifts by saying, "Hailing frequencies open," in honor of Uhura. Jemison even appeared in an episode of *Star Trek: The Next Generation* as Lieutenant Palmer!

"It is useful to distinguish among four factors which give importance, urgency, and inevitability to the advancement of space technology. The first of these factors is the compelling urge of man to explore and to discover, the thrust of curiosity that leads men to try to go where no one has gone before." Sound familiar? Those last few words inspired the now-famous "to boldly go where no man has gone before" opening sequence of the original *Star Trek* television show. They were originally taken from *Introduction to Outer Space*, a 1958 booklet written by a presidential advisory group working to promote the cause of space exploration in the United States after Sputnik's launch. When Gene Roddenberry brought *Star Trek* to television, much of his futuristic vision was influenced by space exploration and happenings on Earth during the turbulent 1960s. With its multiracial and multiethnic cast and characters, and storylines that addressed issues of discrimination and warfare, *Star Trek* has often been called groundbreaking. There was a Russian crew member added during its second season to bring attention to the Cold War. Today, the *Star Trek* universe includes films, spinoff shows, and more. Nichelle Nichols, who was cast as Lieutenant Uhura in the original series, was notable for her portrayal of a professional at a time when black actors were often restricted to roles as servants. Martin Luther King Jr. was a *Star Trek* fan and convinced Nichols to remain on the show. In an interview on NPR, Nichols remembered meeting King: "I think I said something like, 'Dr. King, I wish I could be out there marching with you.' He said, 'No, no, no. No, you don't understand. We don't need you on the—to march. You are marching. You are reflecting what we are fighting for.'"

Actress Whoopi Goldberg, who appeared on *Star Trek: The Next Generation* as Guinan, has spoken often of Nichols's influencial presence on the show. Nichols recalls show creator Roddenberry telling her that Goldberg was "nutty over *Star Trek*." When asked why, Goldberg reportedly told Roddenberry, "It's all Nichelle Nichols's fault . . . she was a black woman playing in the future, and I knew we had a future . . . I knew that I could be anything that I wanted to be." Actor and literacy advocate LeVar Burton, who played Geordie La Forge on *The Next Generation*, also directed several episodes in the franchise. La Forge was blind, and Burton says that, "People . . . dealing with physical challenges . . . tell me how important it was to see themselves represented on that spaceship." Though it was hard to portray on screen, Burton said in an interview that "Geordie . . . was supposed to be able to see everything that nobody else could." Many believe that the inclusiveness of shows like *Star Trek* helped move real-world culture forward. "By telling these stories . . . that's what *Star Trek* represents to people: When the future comes, there's a place for you."

FUN FACT Nichelle Nichols worked as a NASA recruiter in the 1980s, encouraging African Americans and women to join the agency. She even flew on a mission that analyzed the atmospheres of Mars and Venus.

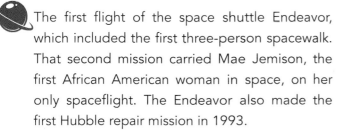

ORION NEBULA
1400 LIGHT-YEARS

Despite budget cuts and challenges, NASA's spirit of exploration stayed strong. In the 1990s, we saw:

 The Magellan mission to Venus in 1990 that showed evidence of volcanic activity on that planet.

 The 1990 launch (and 1993 repair) of the Hubble Space Telescope. Even with its hiccups, the Hubble has helped us confirm the existence of black holes and understand the birth and death of stars even as it continues to offer us spectacular views of space.

The first flight of the space shuttle Endeavor, which included the first three-person spacewalk. That second mission carried Mae Jemison, the first African American woman in space, on her only spaceflight. The Endeavor also made the first Hubble repair mission in 1993.

Russian cosmonaut Sergei Krikalev joining astronauts Charles Bolden and Kenneth Reightler Jr. on the space shuttle Discovery, becoming the first Russian on a US space mission in 1994.

Twenty years after the big Apollo-Soyuz space handshake, the space shuttle Atlantis docked to the Mir space station in 1995—the US and Russian space programs were reunited.

At a cost of $267 million, the Mars Pathfinder spacecraft had been made on the cheap, but in this case, scientists got a whole lot of bang for their bucks. Landing on Mars on July 4, 1997, with its little robotic rover named Sojourner, Pathfinder started collecting data. And it kept going. And going. And going. Scientists learned more about Mars's atmosphere, geology, and weather than they'd ever expected. The Pathfinder mission generated more than 10,000 images of Mars—that would make quite a social media feed! In fact, individuals were able to see images that NASA posted to the Internet and be a part of the experience.

In 1996 and 1997, the Galileo space probe, launched in 1989 and arriving on Jupiter in 1995, produced images that showed possible "ice floes" and icebergs on Jupiter's Europa moon, as well as areas that looked like they might contain water. Signs of a possibility of life! NASA historians write that "many scientists and science-fiction writers have speculated that Europa—in addition to Mars and one of Saturn's moons, Titan—is one of the three planetary bodies in this solar system that might possess, or may have possessed, an environment where primitive life can exist."

The 1997 Mars Cassini-Huygens mission to Saturn was a three-way partnership between NASA, the European Space Agency, and the Italian Space Agency. Cassini launched on October 15, 1997, and took seven years to get to Saturn. As Ethan Siegal wrote in *Forbes*, the Cassini spacecraft, with its Huygens probe, discovered: new Saturnian moons, including one, Encelaedus, that has the three ingredients for potential life ("water, warmth, and organic molecules"); gaps in the planet's rings; a "polar storm" whirling around its north pole; and more.

In September 1997, the Mars Global Surveyor (MGS) space probe helped to finally debunk one of the lasting Mars myths. In 1976, images from the Viking had shown what looked like a face on Mars—and it really did resemble a human face staring up from the red planet.

Conspiracy theorists had been buzzing about it for decades. The higher resolution MGS proved once and for all that the "face" was just a trick of light. MGS also collected data that suggested the possibility of climate change on Mars.

While the new space station was being built, US space shuttles continued to operate in different ways. Astronaut Shannon Lucid, a member of NASA's first astronaut class to include women, flew on the Atlantis to the Russian space station Mir. Lucid spent 188 days aboard the Mir—the only American woman to have lived and worked on the Russian space station. In 1998, former Mercury astronaut John Glenn brought a spirit of hope and joy to young and old alike (but especially old), when he returned to space on the Discovery at age 77, becoming the oldest person to fly in space. He went on to become a US senator for Ohio before passing away in 2016.

Also in 1998, the United States joined 14 other countries in signing the Intergovernmental Agreement on Space Station Cooperation. NASA's Lynn Cline, who helped manage the negotiations between the countries, said, "What I hope it will have as a legacy for the future is that it's a stepping-stone in research, in human spaceflight, in evolution to the next step." And with a renewed sense of hope for the future of NASA and its work, an American-Russian team began living on the ISS in November 2000.

DRY RIVERBED ON MARS
PHOTO BY NASA'S CURIOSITY ROVER

SPOTLIGHT: ELLEN OCHOA

Ellen Ochoa didn't exactly grow up dreaming about space travel. "Women weren't accepted into the [NASA] Astronaut Corps until I was halfway through college, so I hadn't considered it as a career when I was young," she said in an interview. Ochoa did play the flute and considered majoring in music in college. She was also interested in engineering, then decided to major in physics after someone told her that engineering was "not a woman's field."

In spite of that, Ochoa decided to study engineering in graduate school and got interested in looking at how computers "see," designing optical information systems. She went on to invent object-recognition technology used in robotics. "You might use that on a manufacturing line if you're trying to inspect equipment and you're looking for defects," she says. "Or you might use it on an autonomous lander to Mars when you're trying to land around a particular spot and you're using a video camera to look for it. And you can use optics to help you find the right place. Those were the kinds of things I was looking for and those were what some of my patents are in."

After three tries, Ochoa was admitted into NASA's astronaut program and made her first trip into space on the Discovery in 1993, studying the ozone layer and working on the shuttle's robotic arm. Ochoa is of Mexican heritage and was the first Latina in space. She went on three more missions and spent a total of almost 1,000 hours among the stars!

Despite that, she never forgot about her music. On her very first shuttle flight, she brought her flute along and played in the zero-gravity environment. Today, Ellen Ochoa is director of Johnson Space Center, breaking more ground as the first Latina and second woman to hold the position. "Don't be afraid to reach for the stars," she says. "I believe a good education can take you anywhere on Earth and beyond."

chapter seven
OVERCOMING CHALLENGES

REALLY HAUTE COUTURE AND BOTTOMLESS RUNWAYS: SPACESUITS AND SPACEWALKS

WHAT'S UP WITH THE ORANGE SUITS?

THE PRECURSORS to spacesuits were designed for pilots who needed protection from the subzero temperatures in high altitudes—or else they'd end up unconscious. When you're in high altitudes, you have to worry about oxygen levels and pressure falling; it can be deadly. "Full-pressure" suits were built like giant people-shaped bags; they would inflate if the cockpit depressurized and automatically deflate once the planes reached an altitude low enough.

There was a time when space-age fashion was a thing, but orange wasn't meant to be a fashion statement when it became the spacesuit uniform color. At one time, astronauts wore white suits, but in the space shuttle era, things got way brighter and stayed that way. The color of the suits that astronauts wear on the space shuttle is officially called International Orange, and it was chosen because it stands out, which makes it great for safety. "It's highly visible for search and rescue," says NASA's Brian Daniel on LiveScience.com. "It's one of the most visible colors, especially for sea rescue."

The suits are called ACES—advanced crew escape suits—and they're like the Swiss Army knife of spacewear: They come equipped with a water supply, radio, flares, a parachute, and more.

When astronauts go on spacewalks, they do a not-so-quick change into the bulkier white *extra-vehicular activity* (EVA) suits. White reflects the Sun and stands out in the black expanse of space. NASA developed these EVA suits to do a lot more than just look a little funny. They're called *extravehicular mobility units* (EMUs) and are even poofier than the ACES. There are 14 layers of protection between an astronaut and space. NASA says its EMUs are "really a small spacecraft." They control temperature, contain breathable air and drinkable water, and have a tough shell to prevent small pieces of space junk, like micrometeoroids, from harming the astronauts.

The Department of Defense US Space Surveillance Network is tracking about half a million pieces of "space junk," from tiny 1/2-inch pieces to some pieces that are larger than 4 inches wide, reports LiveScience.com. Pieces of satellites and rockets, often left over from crashes in space, make up the bulk of this debris. "Such crashes, and their ensuing additions to the swarm of junk in space, will only become more common as space gets even more crowded."

Here's what else those puffy suits have got going on:

 They start with, well . . . a diaper. Officially called a *maximum absorbency garment*, or MAG, these superduper absorbent undies are pulled on like shorts and worn during liftoff, landing, and EVAs, like spacewalks. These superdiapers contain a white powder called *sodium polyacrylate* that can absorb up to 1,000 times its mass in water.

 The "Snoopy cap," named for the *Peanuts* character because of its black and white design, is a helmet equipped with microphones and ear-pieces for communication.

 Then there's a cooling suit, the *liquid cooling and ventilation garment* (LCVG). It's equipped with tubes that transport water through the suit and help keep the astronaut cool. It can get sizzling hot in there!

 There's a hard, upper part of the suit that goes on the torso. It holds a 32-ounce bag of drinking water (gotta stay hydrated!). And then there's the flexible, lower leg portion. Attached to the back is a backpack—but it doesn't carry textbooks and a brown bag lunch. Rather, it holds lifesaving tools and supplies. These *primary life support systems* (PLSS) have an oxygen tank, batteries, and the cooling water that runs through the LCVG tubes.

Connected to the front of the suit is a display-and-control module that allows the astronaut to control all of the suit's systems. The control labels are written backward—astronauts use a mirror attached to their wrists to read them!

The outer shell of the suit is made of tough stuff in order to prevent bits of space junk from hurting the astronauts.

The hard helmet holds oxygen for breathing and removes carbon dioxide through the backpack. Then a special visor goes over the helmet, protecting the astronaut's eyes from the Sun and providing cameras and spotlights to help them do their work.

Though they look light and floaty, all of this means that the suits are super heavy! "The spacesuit itself weighs about 400 pounds on Earth" astronaut and US Air Force Colonel Terry Virts told NPR. "And so moving around in the spacesuit . . . requires physical exertion."

SPACEWALKING

"To space-walk out there is a great experience. You're hanging onto a bar, you know, like a commuter. And with just sort of a power tool in the other hand. It's an achievement."
—Piers Sellers, former director of Earth Science at NASA

Astronauts can't just jump into their suits and float out into space. Before an astronaut even goes on a spacewalk, they'll have done at least five "practice runs" on Earth. On the ground, they prepare by swimming. Because floating in space is a little like floating in water, astronauts practice at NASA's Neutral Buoyancy Laboratory in Houston. It's a giant pool that holds about 6.2 million gallons of water! Astronauts do seven hours of pool training for every hour of planned spacewalking. They also play video games . . . sort of. They're equipped with a virtual-reality helmet that simulates the space environment and they use special gloves to navigate.

Gemini 4 astronaut Ed White was the first NASA astronaut to spacewalk, in 1965, for a total of 23 minutes.

The US record is currently held by Michael Lopez-Alegria, who walked for more than 67 hours over a total of 10 spacewalks. Currently, spacewalks are about 5–8 hours long.

It was during swim practice that Leland Melvin almost lost his opportunity to ever go to space. Melvin, the "only person drafted into the National Football League to have flown into space," grew up admiring tennis legend Arthur Ashe, but instead of tennis, Melvin was a part of the Detroit Lions and Dallas Cowboys teams until injuries got in the way. With a bachelor's degree in chemistry and a graduate degree in materials-science engineering, Melvin went on to work for NASA at the Langley Research Center. Melvin didn't plan to be an astronaut, but after a friend was accepted into the program, Melvin saw that "he was flying jets . . . inspiring kids, he was going to be flying in space one day . . . that's the ultimate gig." In an appearance on *CBS This Morning*, he remembered that after another friend was accepted, he also told himself, "If that knucklehead could get in, I can get in!" He joined the NASA Astronauts Corps in 1998, but one day, as he was being lowered into the training pool, "I realized that this little Styrofoam pad was not in my helmet," he said in an interview with *The Verge*. "They forgot to put mine in . . . from that point on, I heard nothing but static." Melvin lost his hearing due to the lack of proper ear protection; for a while doctors couldn't help, and it seemed like his dreams of space travel were over. He slowly regained some of his hearing, though he remains hearing-impaired in one ear. Still inter-

ested in inspiring young people, Melvin went on to work for NASA's education department, traveling the country to visit schools and promote STEM education.

Melvin lost friends in the space shuttle Columbia tragedy. The father of one of the victims, David Brown, reminded him of the importance of carrying on the Columbia crew's legacy and moving forward with space travel. Melvin was still medically disqualified from space flight, "But as we fly around the country to go the different memorial services, the chief flight surgeon . . . says, 'I'm going to sign you a waiver to fly. This will be your testimony to the world.'" Melvin went on to fly twice as a mission specialist on the space shuttle Atlantis to the ISS. Today, the boy whose early science experiments "created an explosion" in his family living room believes that his NFL training was instrumental to his success as an astronaut. "That teamwork, that dedication, that discipline . . . helped model me for the astronaut training program," he said on CBS. Melvin tells his story in the book *Chasing Space: An Astronaut's Story of Grit, Grace, and Second Chances*. "My mission is to take the experiences that I had in space, seeing this incredible planet . . . and bring that down to the classroom, so the kids can say, 'Wow, I can do that! And that guy looks kinda like me—maybe I can be an astronaut!'"

On the spacecraft, it takes about four hours just to put the whole suit on and make sure that everything's working and ready to go. Then . . . they're off! Sort of.

On spacewalks, astronauts are tethered to their spacecraft on thin cords, like leashes, so that they don't just float away. Their tools are also tethered to their spacesuits. Every moment of a spacewalk is carefully planned—no impromptu strolls or air-guitar time is allowed. If an astronaut needs to be rescued,

a mobile spacecraft can move into position to help them out. In the space shuttle era, astronauts had jet-powered backpacks as well. But those are no longer in use, and something stationary, like the ISS, can't move into position to help out an astronaut in trouble. If an astronaut does somehow become unhooked, a SAFER can shoot them back to safety. A SAFER, which is basically like a life-saving jet pack, is a small and light pack that attaches to the suit and uses nitrogen-powered jets and a hand controller to help the astronaut move back to the station. NASA engineers are currently working on something even simpler called a Take Me Home system that would activate an astronaut's automatic return at the push of a button—some believe that the technology used to develop this system could also help scuba divers, firefighters, and others in their work here on Earth.

Spacewalkers are often carried by robotic arms, like the Canadarm2, the Canadian tool that helped put the ISS together and is used to carry and move equipment, supplies, and people.

Astronaut Scott Kelly joked that spacewalking is a far cry from a walk in the park. "Still trying to wrap my head around why we call it #spacewalk, not space-work," he tweeted. Douglas Wheelock, aka "Wheels," has been on six spacewalks and agrees. He told *National Geographic*, "You propel yourself, you stop yourself, you hold on to things with your fingertips, and you just kind of push off and just get yourself stable with your fingertips." Astronauts' hands and forearms get pretty sore. "The best thing you could do for your spacewalking fitness is to sit with one of those hand-squeezer things," says Wheels. "You'll have big Popeye arms and strong hands."

"When you're outside the station, you are literally an independent astronomical body, a tiny moon of Earth, orbiting at 17,500 miles an hour," writes Charles Fishman in *The Atlantic*. "When you look at Earth between your boots, that first step is more than one million feet down."

It sure looks like fun, doesn't it? Like being in a bouncy house where you never have to touch the ground. But astronauts are not exactly out there do-ing backflips and taking selfies all day. Virts says that "99.5 percent of . . . my time on my spacewalks, I can say, was completely focused on what was going on . . . There was no time to stop and look around, there's no time to take pictures." On spacewalks, astronauts are working hard, doing things like conducting science experiments and fixing equip-ment. Most of the time is spent repairing and main-taining the ISS.

In space, they prepare for an EVA by putting on their suits and breathing in pure oxygen for a few hours. That gets rid of nitrogen in the body that could cause painful internal gas bubbles while out in space. When they're ready to head out, they go through the airlock, which are two airtight doors that won't open at the same time—one has to be tightly closed be-fore the other will open, minimizing a dangerous loss of air and pressure on the spacecraft.

And sometimes, things can go wrong.

THE INTERNATIONAL SPACE RUNWAY

Russia also has two suits for its cosmonauts, both white. The *Sokol* is for launch and landing and the *Orlan* is for spacewalking. China also has its own spacesuits: the *Feitian*, which was inspired by the Russian Orlan suits; and another for launch and landing that looks like the Sokol.

NASA's Robonaut may someday replace astronaut spacewalks. The prototype now on the ISS can flip switches and may be configured to do EVA work as well.

Q&A WITH NASA ENGINEER ADAM STELTZNER

Q: What are the pros and cons of sending robots into space?

A: Pros: Robots aren't cranky or thirsty or in need of much sleep. They eat very little and usually do not complain. Cons: Robots never write poetry and space is full of poetic inspiration.

HOUSTON . . . ANOTHER PROBLEM

In 2013, Italian ISS astronaut Luca Parmitano almost drowned on his second spacewalk. His cooling suit leaked when he was upside down; it started flooding his helmet with water. He didn't want to let the team on the ground in Houston know that he was having a problem, but he told them what was going on—for a little while. The water instantly turned to a gel-like substance, breaking Parmitano's communication system. And then the Sun went down. "I couldn't hear anything anymore. I couldn't see anything anymore," he told NPR. "And I couldn't breathe through my nose. Because my nose was filled up with water."

Breathing through his mouth, Parmitano felt his way back to the spacecraft, unhappy but unharmed. And undeterred. "I wanted to go out the next day." After the scary incident, NASA added absorbent pads to astronauts' helmets. In a blog post, Parmitano wrote a sobering reminder of the unpredictable nature of space exploration. "Space is a harsh, inhospitable frontier, and we are explorers, not colonizers. The skills of our engineers and the technology surrounding us make things appear simple when they are not, and perhaps we forget this sometimes.

"Better not to forget."

In general, "aquanauts" are people who live and work underwater for more than 24-hour periods. Did you know that NASA has its own team of aquanauts? The NASA Extreme Environment Mission Operations (NEEMO) project sends astronauts, scientists, and engineers to live in the world's only underwater research center: Aquarius, located in the Florida Keys National Marine Sanctuary. The deep seas are considered "hostile," like space; aquanauts experience many challenges that are similar to what they'd experience on a distant planet. And no, they're not just *really* good at holding their breath. Aquanauts use a technique called "saturation diving." They remain in the water at a certain depth until their body tissues are saturated with the gases that they breathe. Once

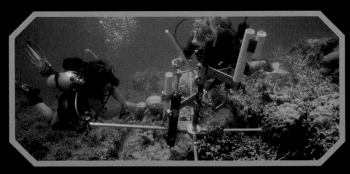

NASA reef team collects data.

their body saturation is the same as the pressure of the surrounding water, they can stay underwater for long periods of time and minimize the risk of illness. With Project NEEMO, NASA is able to study the habitability of an extreme environment (the deep seas) and develop technology for future space exploration.

DID YOU KNOW: Luca Parmitano has an asteroid named after him, called 37627 Lucaparmitano.

PROFILE: MARY GOLDA ROSS

Some hidden heroines avoid the spotlight on purpose, and others must avoid it because of the nature of their work. For Mary Golda Ross, it was a little bit of both. The name of the woman who wrote NASA's guide to space travel, the *Planetary Flight Handbook*, and worked on early concepts for missions to Venus and Mars is not well-known, but the impact of her work is legendary. Recognized as the first Native American female engineer, Ross's Cherokee heritage included the forced relocation of her ancestors. Born in 1908 in Oklahoma (just a year after the state itself was born), Ross showed an early aptitude for math. "Math was more fun than anything else," she's quoted as saying, even though often "I was the only female in my class. I sat on one side of the room and the guys [were] on the other side of the room. I guess they didn't want to associate with me. But I could hold my own with them and sometimes did better." She went on to earn a bachelor's degree in math at 20 years old, taught high school for a number of years, and earned a master's degree from the University of Oklahoma, "where she took every astronomy class they had." During the Great Depression, Ross taught math and science in rural Oklahoma and worked with Native American children at a boarding school in New Mexico.

Ross was hired as a mathematician by Lockheed Martin, a consultant to NASA. "I was the pencil pusher, doing a lot of research. My state-of-the-art tools were a slide rule and a Friden computer," she said in an interview with the *San Jose Mercury News*. "We were taking the theoretical and making it real." Her work prompted the company to send her to UCLA for a professional certification in engineering, and after that she returned to Lockheed Martin, joining a program called Skunk Works. She worked on the Apollo Program, interplanetary space travel concepts, the Agena rocket project, and more. She was the only woman in Lockheed's Missiles Systems Division researching national-defense systems. There isn't much detail available about her work, because it's still *classified*, meaning it's top-secret. In 1958, she appeared on the television show *What's My Line?*, where contestants had to guess the participants' careers. In part because she couldn't answer certain questions that related to the top-secret nature of her work and largely because of her gender, it took a very long time for the players to guess that Mary Golda Ross was someone who "designs rocket missiles and satellites." Ross was modest about her accomplishments and often stressed collaboration as a reason for much of her success. "I have always considered my work a joint effort," she said. "I was fortunate to have worked on great ideas and with very intelligent people. I may have developed a few equations no one had thought of before, but that was nothing unusual—everybody did that."

Ross became involved with the American Indian Science and Engineering Society and the Council of Energy Resource Tribes. "There is a lot of ancient wisdom from Indian culture that would help solve the problems of today," she said.

After she retired, Ross made speeches across the country, encouraging young women and Native youth to pursue engineering careers. When she was 96, she participated in the opening ceremonies of the National Museum of the American Indian in Washington, DC, proudly wearing ancestral Cherokee clothing made by her niece. Remembered as "an innovative, methodical, systematic analyst who never relaxed her efforts on a task until it was completed" by a colleague, Ross died in 2008, just before her hundredth birthday. She often remembered her time with NASA planning space missions as her favorite work. "Compared to the classified research, it was a lot more fun since you could talk about it," she explained in an interview. "I consider myself extremely fortunate to have been on the ground floor of space technology."

CHAPTER EIGHT

NO MORE MONKEY BUSINESS

THE HISTORY OF ANIMALS IN SPACE AND PLAY AS SERIOUS BUSINESS

IN THE NAME OF SCIENCE, there have been attempts to launch nonhuman animals into space for a very long time. Scientists wondered about the effects of space travel on the human body, and according to NASA, "For several years, there had been a serious debate among scientists about the effects of prolonged weightlessness," so rodents, primates, dogs, and more were utilized by both the United States and Soviet Union to get answers.

The first animals in space probably weren't exactly missed by their human neighbors. Fruit flies were launched in a Nazi V-2 rocket, went up 68 miles, and were later recovered alive and well. A series of monkeys, all named Albert (I–IV) were launched

between 1948 and 1950. They did not fare as well; none survived their flights. Several attempts to launch mice also ended in the animals' deaths.

Finally, on September 20, 1951, a monkey named Yorick and his 11 mouse friends were launched 236,000 feet into the sky—and made it back. The triumph was short-lived; Yorick and two of the mice died a few hours after landing.

Patricia and Mike, two Philippine primates, had a better outcome; in order to test the effects of rapid acceleration, Patricia was placed in a seated position while Mike lay flat. Both survived the 36-mile flight into the sky.

Two white mice, Mildred and Albert, who

traveled with them in a slowly rotating drum also survived. NASA launched the Mouse In Able (MIA) project in 1958, and most of the mice did not survive, including Wilkie, who was lost at sea.

During the '50s, the Soviets made many attempts at launching dogs into space, believing that they would be "less fidgety" in flight. Stray dogs were often used because scientists felt they would be accustomed to extreme cold. Many, like famed Sputnik 2 dog, Laika, died. But in 1966, cosmodogs Veterok (which means "breeze" in English) and Ugolyok ("little piece of coal") orbited the Earth for 22 days and landed safely—a canine space travel record that remains standing today. (Humans broke that record in 1974, on Skylab 2.)

One year after Laika's fateful flight, the United States launched a squirrel monkey named Gordo, who perished when his flotation mechanism failed on splashdown. Rhesus monkeys Sam and his mate, Miss Sam, had a better experience. These primates, whose names were acronyms for US Air Force School of Aviation Medicine at Brooks Air Force Base, Texas,

were launched and landed safely, both returning to their training colonies for long periods afterward.

Ham, whose name was an acronym for Holloman Aero Med, was the first chimpanzee in space, flying in style in a Mercury-Redstone rocket at the end of January in 1961. Ham flew higher and farther than expected, but after a 16 ¹/₂-minute flight—during which he experienced 6 ¹/₂ minutes of weightlessness—he landed safely, dehydrated and tired but generally okay. Ham's flight paved the way for Alan Shepard's historic launch on May 5, 1961. After his flight, Ham was sent to Washington's National Zoo in 1963, where he remained until his death in 1980.

It wasn't until 1961 that the first chimp successfully orbited the Earth. Enos launched on November 29 of that year, aboard a Mercury Atlas rocket. He landed after two orbits in good condition. This was the final (and successful) test mission in preparation for John Glenn's orbital flight in 1962.

France did things a little differently, launching a cat named Félicette (sometimes inelegantly nicknamed "Astrocat") 100 miles into the air in 1963. The black-and-white stray went through a number of

compression and centrifugal chamber tests, along with 13 other cats, in preparation for her trip. The test cats all had electrodes implanted in their brains so that scientists could record their brain activity, so though Félicette survived her trip, she was euthanized a few months later so that scientists could study the effects of space travel on her body. Her legacy survives on stamps, and in 2017, an artist ran a successful crowdfunding campaign to create a memorial in her honor.

Nonhuman animals in space stopped being a "thing" once humans made successful Moon landings. In the 1980s, spacecraft continued to carry *payloads* (or cargo and passengers) with living creatures like turtles, rabbits, roundworms, spiders, fish, insects, jellyfish, and more. We've learned that not all species develop typically in weightlessness, which is something we would probably never have been able to know without transporting animals to space. For instance, frog eggs successfully hatched into tadpoles, but the organ in crickets that affects their balance doesn't develop properly. Using crickets in an experiment allowed scientists to see significant organ development over a short period of time.

NASA and other space agencies' animals-in-space endeavors are not meant to be mere stunts. Though most early studies were focused on whether or not humans would be able to survive in space and on the effects of space travel on the body, later experiments have investigated issues affecting us here on Earth. "Rodent-testing in space serves the same purpose as rodent-testing on the ground," writes author Calla Cofield on Space.com, "and is frequently a step toward a new treatment or medicine to help humans . . . Today, animal tests are helping scientists prepare

for the hazards that humans will face if they ever want to visit Mars or live on the surface of the Moon for prolonged periods of time." Fruit flies are used to study the effects of space radiation; NASA and other countries' agencies have rodent habitats on the ISS; and the Japanese space agency has an aquarium. "We're always going to be looking for the simplest organism we can fly that will answer a scientific question," said Brad Carpenter, chief scientist for NASA's Space Life and Physical Sciences Research and Applications Division. "We have an ethical obligation, and we have policy and regulation that require [it]. We can't inappropriately use a vertebrate organism for research."

TOYS IN SPACE

In the name of science education, four space shuttle missions have brought a total of 66 toys into space, giving students the opportunity to learn about the laws of physics as they saw how toys behaved in

Earth's gravity versus the microgravity environment in space.

Other toys have made their way on a few missions, but just as passengers—not for science.

A photo of an experiment being conducted on the International Space Station.

In addition to being a flight engineer, astronaut Karen Nyberg is a crafter—she sewed a dinosaur in space! She brought sewing needles, a few fabric scraps, and some thread along with her as a member of Expedition 36 on the ISS. Once onboard, she found a few other items to make a plush dinosaur. "It is made out of Velcro-like fabric that lines the Russian food containers found here on the International Space Station," Nyberg wrote. "It is lightly stuffed with scraps from a used T-shirt." Nyberg made the dinosaur as a gift for her then three-year-old son, Jack. This first stuffed animal made in space joined a stuffed white dog and black cat, which were brought onboard by other crew members.

Sometimes stuffed animals serve a purpose. Astronauts hang small toys on launch to show them when weightlessness is achieved—they know they've hit microgravity when the toy floats. Cosmonaut Yuri Gagarin was the first to do this, on Vostok 1. "The tradition of carrying small toys as weightless indicators dates back to the very first time a human was launched into space," space historian Robert Pearlman told Mashable.

Along with a small Puerto Rican flag, NASA astronaut Joe Acaba—the first astronaut candidate of Puerto Rican descent—brought a stuffed "Smokey the Bear" on Expedition 31 to the ISS. Smokey was a gift from a friend in the US Forest Service and an appropriate one for Acaba, who worked in environmental education and holds degrees in geology.

Other stuffed toys in space include Olaf the snowman from the film *Frozen*, an Angry Bird, and a hippopotamus in a spacesuit!

FUN AND GAMES ARE SERIOUS BUSINESS
LONNIE JOHNSON AND THE SUPER SOAKER

The Super Soaker toy is one of the most popular toys around and is a billion-dollar phenomenon and best-seller around the world. Did you know that a NASA engineer invented it? Lonnie Johnson first thought of the "power drencher" while he was serving in the US Air Force. But his passion for engineering started long before. "It started with my dad," Johnson said in an interview with the BBC. "He gave me my first lesson in electricity, explaining that it takes two wires for an electric current to flow—one for the electrons to go in, the other for them to come out. And he showed me how to repair irons and lamps and things like that."

From there Johnson went on to take apart his sister's doll, to see how the eye-closing mechanism worked, and to try building a robot like the ones he saw on TV (he didn't realize that those were played by actors). But Johnson, a young black man whose friends called him "the Professor" while growing up in segregated Mobile, Alabama, didn't stop. He finished his robot, called Linex, and entered it into a local science competition at the University of Alabama—which he won. "We were the only black school there. This was 1968 . . . my high school was in the news a lot because they were integrating us. White people were coming on TV, calling us all kinds of names and saying they didn't want their kids coming to the school and being exposed to us."

Johnson's success attracted the attention of the air force and Tuskegee University. He went to Tuskegee on an air force scholarship and got bachelor's and master's degrees in mechanical and nuclear engineering. In the air force, Johnson worked on nuclear-powered space launches by day and tinkered with developing cooling systems that used water instead of chlorofluorocarbons, which destroyed the environment. "One evening, I machined a nozzle and hooked it up to the bathroom sink, where I was performing some experiments. It shot a powerful stream of water across the bathroom sink. That's when I got the idea that a powerful water gun would be fun!"

Johnson continued his air force duties, working on the stealth-bomber program and at NASA's Jet Propulsion Laboratory. He fiddled with his idea and built a prototype in his basement. It was a success with his daughter, and even his colleagues got into the fun at social events. Johnson went on to partner with a toy company to mass-produce the invention, first calling it the Power Drencher before settling on Super Soaker. Today there are a number of different models that use different piston pumper, air-pressure, and spring-powered systems to operate. The Super Soaker was inducted into the National Toy Hall of Fame in 2015.

The Super Soaker has not been without controversy. Sometimes people have used them in inappropriate ways. When a politician tried to have them banned, Johnson was asked what he thought. "In the back of my mind, I felt that my work on toy guns was probably less harmful than the work I did on real weapons systems," said Johnson.

Johnson retired from NASA and now runs a scientific company in Georgia, where, among other things, he studies battery technology and affordable "green" energy. Johnson has gone on to patent many more inventions, including a "wet-diaper detector." He was inducted into Alabama's Engineering Hall of Fame in 2011—the first African American to receive that honor.

FOMALHAUT B
25 LIGHT-YEARS

Discovered in 2008, Fomalhaut (also known as Dragon) is approximately 25 light-years from the constellation Piscis Austrinus. Photo taken by the Hubble Telescope.

CHAPTER NINE
MAKING IMPOSSIBLE REAL

STAR TREK, STAR WARS . . . EARTHSTAR? WHAT HAPPENS WHEN SCIENCE FICTION AND SCIENCE CONVERGE?

WHY IS DARTH VADER'S BREATHING SO WEIRD?

IT'S NOT UNUSUAL FOR scientists and researchers to use popular culture as a teaching tool. So when two Denmark physicians set out to diagnose the evil space lord of *Star Wars* in a study snappily called "Pulmonary Pathophysiology in Another Galaxy," they weren't laughed out of their field. *National Geographic* reports that Ronan M. G. Berg and Ronni R. Plovsing did a scene-by-scene analysis of Vader's breathing patterns and concluded that he had probably breathed in the gases and volcanic particles on the planet Mustafar (where he fought and fell to Obi-Wan Kenobi). "Darth Vader may be considered an example of acute and chronic respiratory failure following severe burns and thermal lung injury," the doctors report. The burning-hot gases would have left Vader's lungs "chronically inflamed, with tissue thickened and stiffened by scarring." Berg says that this situation would mean

that Vader's famous black robes are a "wearable hyperbaric chamber, designed to force air into his lungs." If Berg had his way, he says he'd just go with a lung transplant.

can Robots Be OUR Best FRIenDS anD clean OUR ROOMS?

Author and professor of biochemistry Isaac Asimov made robots sympathetic in his short story "Robbie," and from C-3PO and R2-D2 to BB-8, the *Star Wars* universe has no shortage of droids with an abundance of personality and skill. Can we make robots that behave the same way? That's probably a long way off. It's hard to make robots that think the way we do, because there's a whole lot we don't know about our own brains. *Forbes* magazine reports that a company based in Japan called Softbank is planning to sell "affectionate robots" that are "programmed to read the emotions of people around it by recognizing expressions and voice tones."

Engineers are currently working on the development of an all-robot soccer team. *Smithsonian* reports that the goal is that by the 2050s, they will have created "a team of fully autonomous humanoid robot soccer players [that can] win a soccer game, complying with the official rules of FIFA, against the winner of the most recent World Cup."

So far companies have developed robots that can do simple tasks like greet patrons, and NASA is in the process of developing robots that might actually take the place of human astronauts in space travel. The 300-pound, six-foot-two-inch robot named Robonaut 5 (R5 for short, and formerly known as Valkyrie) was built by engineers at the Johnson Space Center. It looks a little like Iron Man. R5 can run on batteries or be plugged into an electrical outlet. According to NASA, "As missions grow longer and more complex, robots like R5 could be used as precursor explorers that precede crewed missions, as crew helpers in space, or as caretakers of assets left behind." Robots could one day be greeting us when we arrive on Mars!

OKay, so can we JUST Be ROBOTS OURSeLVeS? WILL BIONIC LIMBS GIVe US SUPeRPOWeRS?

We can't point to superpowers, but there is a device nicknamed the "LUKE Arm"—it enables an amputee to use their mind to control the prosthesis. Whoa! Mind control sounds pretty amazing. Named for the cool robotic arm that Luke Skywalker got at the end of *The Empire Strikes Back*, it works by using electrodes that connect the device to the nervous system. Maybe "mind control" is exaggerating? Mashable describes it this way: "Electrodes let the wearer control the LUKE Arm's movements with muscle movements and the device transmits grip feedback to the user through a grip-force sensor."

Still: pretty cool. Developed by Dean Kamen, the man who also invented the Segway, in partnership with the Defense Advanced Research Projects Agency (DARPA), the LUKE Arm is a whole new level of prosthetic technology. It has motors in more than one place—the hand, the shoulder, and elbow—so that wearers have more flexibility and an ability to handle large and small objects.

ROBOTS are COOL, BUT a LIGHT SABER WOULD BE amazing . . .

Well, the military has been thinking the same thing. The armed forces have been working with lithium-ion battery, technology-powered laser prototypes that could possibly be in use by the 2020s. Not many details are available—it's classified information. The air force is also developing a sorta-kinda light saber called the TEC Torch—it's not able to extend as far as a light saber, but it burns hotter than 4,000°F and generates enough heat to slice right through a metal door lock.

Can we just have our own STAR WARS in SPACE now?

When President Barack Obama's administration launched its We the People petitioning program in 2011, it probably didn't expect 34,435 people to request the construction of a Death Star, the *Star Wars* space station that could basically annihilate entire planets. But the petition, created in 2012, pointed out that "by focusing our defense resources into a space-superiority platform and weapon system such as a Death Star, the government can spur job creation in the fields of construction, engineering, space exploration, and more, and strengthen our national defense."

The White House was unconvinced, laying out a number of reasons for a big NO WAY:

"The administration shares your desire for job creation and a strong national defense, but a Death Star isn't on the horizon. Here are a few reasons:

The construction of the Death Star has been estimated to cost more than $850 quadrillion. We're working hard to reduce the deficit, not expand it.

🪐 The administration does not support blowing up planets.

🪐 Why would we spend countless taxpayer dollars on a Death Star with a fundamental flaw that can be exploited by a one-man starship?"

The response went on to point out that we have something probably cooler and certainly much more productive already in space: the ISS.

IT WOULD BE AWESOME IF BIKES COULD FLY. CAN WE AT LEAST MAKE *THAT* HAPPEN?

The *Star Wars* films sure make it look easy with everyone gliding above the sand as they zip from place to place. We're not quite there yet, but there is a hoverbike on the way, courtesy of the US Defense Department. A successful 2017 demo of the "large rectangular prototype quadcopter"—its official name is Joint Tactical Aerial Resupply Vehicle (JTARV)—in Maryland brought the military closer to the possibility of using hoverbikes to carry supplies to the battlefield.

STAR TREK: A SCIENTIFIC START, A FICTIONAL FINISH

"Original producer Gene Roddenberry and the later writers of the show started with science we know and s-t-r-e-t-c-h-e-d it to fit a framework of amazing inventions that support action-filled and entertaining stories," says David Allen Batchelor, a NASA physicist. So what ended up being a prediction and what remains "out of this world"?

WOULD A TWENTY-FIRST CENTURY E.T. FINALLY BE ABLE TO PHONE HOME?

Resembling those flip phones that are now considered old-school by many in the US, *Star Trek* communicators were a voice-communication-and-emergency-signal system that allowed for communication without needing a satellite. *Star Trek* personnel also used videoconferencing, wristwatch communicators, and iPad-like tablets called PADDs (personal access display devices). "[The iPad's] geometry is almost exactly the same—the corner radius, the thickness, and overall rectangular shape," says *Star Trek* artist Doug Drexler in *Forbes* magazine. "It's uncanny to have a PADD that really works . . . The iPad is the true *Star Trek* dream." The Enterprise crew also used a "universal translator" that was like a superpowered version of the Skype translator software we use now.

ARE WE READY TO BEAT THE HASSLE OF TRADITIONAL AIR TRAVEL BY JUST UTTERING THE WORDS "BEAM ME UP, SCOTTY"?

Not exactly. Teleportation is not a thing yet. But while humans can't do it, scientists in the Netherlands and the US Army have reported success with "quantum teleportation" of information. While the process of processing and transferring enormous amounts of data is still in the earliest stages of development, the *Atlantic* reports that "quantum computing could revolutionize the way we interact with information . . . Such systems would process data faster and on larger scales than even the most super of supercomputers can handle today. But this technology would also dismantle the security systems that institutions like banks and governments use online, which means it matters who gets their hands on a working quantum system first."

Warp Speed Would Really Come in Handy When I've Hit the Snooze Button a Few Too Many Times. How's It Coming?

Sorry, but traveling faster than the speed of light is not possible at the moment; outside of fiction like *A Wrinkle in Time*, we haven't yet figured out how to "tesser" or use a black hole to zip through the (hypothetical) multiverse. But while interstellar travel doesn't seem to be in the near future for humans, NASA's scientists are working on electric-propulsion engines that can move spacecraft into deep space at incredibly high speeds over longer and longer periods of time, and that use small amounts of fuel.

DID YOU KNOW?

John W. Campbell's novel *Islands of Space*, published in 1957, may have had the first mention of "warp drive." The story involved the testing of a ship that moved faster than the speed of light. In a review, award-winning writer Theodore Sturgeon called it "a real lousy book" but ultimately a good thing for the genre.

new narratives

"What really good science fiction does is to allow you to reflect on yourself, your values, and your beliefs . . . It uses a fictionalized science as a mechanism to push us to think about what we're doing. Society is influenced by technology, and the technology is influenced by society, our aspirations, and who we think we are."

—Mae Jemison, first African American woman in space

Many of today's scientists talk of being inspired and encouraged by narratives of fictional worlds in film, television, and books. "Hard" science fiction, by authors like Arthur C. Clarke and Isaac Asimov, focuses heavily on a foundation of scientific accuracy. But from our earliest days, stories have been vehicles for reflection, for understanding our world and our place in it. Though much popular science fiction was not known for its extensive exploration of social issues, writers like Ursula K. Le Guin and Octavia Butler told different stories.

Moving away from the angry little green men on Mars, Le Guin wrote that "imagination, working at full strength, can shake us out of our fatal, adoring self-absorption and make us look up and see—with terror or with relief—that the world does not in fact belong to us at all." In *New Yorker* magazine, Julie Phillips writes that science fiction offered Le Guin "a ready-made set of tools, including spaceships, planets, and aliens, plus a realm— the future—that set no limits on the imagination." Her writing, including well-known works like award-winning *The Left Hand of Darkness* and the **Earthsea** series explore issues of identity and culture along with science. Le Guin, who died in 2018, once told *The Paris Review*, "The 'hard' science-fiction writers dismiss everything except, well, physics, astronomy, and maybe chemistry. Biology, sociology, anthropology—that's not science to them, that's soft stuff. They're not that interested in what human beings do, really. But I am . . . When I create another planet, another world, with a society on it, I try to hint at the complexity of the society I'm creating instead of just referring to an empire or something like that."

Octavia Butler said that it was a bad science-fiction film that drew her to writing. NPR reports that when Butler was nine years old, she saw *Devil Girl from Mars* and thought *Geez, I can write a better story than that!* She also felt surprised that "somebody got *paid* for writing that story!" Though she had always been a writer and story-teller, at that moment, a science-fiction-and-fantasy writer was born.

Butler went on to win a MacArthur "Genius" award and publish 12 novels—stories that endeavored to make readers feel the past, including its pain, and envision a future with new realities. "When I began writing science fiction, when I began reading, heck, I wasn't in any of this stuff I read," Butler told the *New York Times*. "The only black people you found were occasional characters or characters who were so feeble-witted that they couldn't manage anything, anyway. I wrote myself in, since I'm me and I'm here and I'm writing." Books like the time-travel novel *Kindred*, which explored the legacy of American slavery, and *Parable of the Sower*—in which Butler already saw the phenomena of global warming, gated communities, and mistrust between police officers and civilians that we experience now—included social commentary as a vital part of science-fiction storytelling. "When I say these things in my novels," she told the *Times*, "sure, I make up the aliens and all of that, but I don't make up the essential human character."

Though Butler died in 2006, her legacy also lives on in her influence on contemporary science-fiction writers like Tananarive Due. "She was very bothered by humanity's self-destructive tendencies, and so much of her fiction is about trying to help us see the dangers of our present course and trying to present alternatives," Due told CNN. "She wanted us to think and to act, and her passion and prescience really makes her impact timeless."

While much of the stuff of science fiction is still living in our imaginary worlds, Paul Hsieh points out that we're inching closer to realizing the fantastic every day. "MIT has announced a programmable, needle-less medication injector" that delivers medicine in tiny jet sprays like the "hypospray" on *Star Trek* that administered medicine without injection . . . Away from hospitals, emergency and military professionals are already using small hand-held ultrasound scanners like McCoy's tricorder. And with 3-D printers creating LUKE Arms and other replacement body parts, science fiction is becoming fact, offering solutions to some of our most challenging medical issues, and inviting new questions and ideas about the future.

THE WACKY-BUT-TRUE WORLD OF SPACE EXPLORATION

YES, NASA REALLY DOES HAVE AN OFFICIAL "VOMIT COMET"!

When astronaut Scott Tingle's mom asked him to do his "best microgravity trick or flip" in a live satellite conversation with him on the ISS, Tingle's flip looked effortlessly cool. But the truth is that microgravity can make astronauts feel pretty queasy. So preparation involves riding in the "Vomit Comet"—a special aircraft that takes them on a roller coaster–like ride by flying in parabolic arcs to simulate weightlessness. NASA has been working with zero-gravity flight simulators since its early days in the late 1950s, and even civilians like the stars of the film *Apollo 13* and university student researchers have gotten in on the act. "A typical flight will see two to three hours of plunging arcs, giving astronauts about 30 or 40 chances to experience weightlessness when the air-plane drops to a lower altitude. Some researchers also use the flights as a chance to run experiments in weightlessness," reports Elizabeth Howell on LiveScience.com. While the Vomit Comet is a cost-effective way to conduct research, it's not the cleanest. Though sealable barf bags are distributed, when the KC-135 craft was retired from Vomit Comet use in 2004, NASA test director John Yaniac reported that "over the years, the plane's crew had cleaned up at least 285 gallons of vomit." Phys.org reports that "roughly 45 percent of all people who have flown in space have suffered from space sickness. The duration varies, but cases have never been shown to exceed 72 hours, after which the body adapts to the new environment."

NASA WILL PAY ME ALMOST $20,000 TO STAY IN BED?! SIGN ME UP!

Not so fast, lazybones. While it's true that NASA researchers studying weightlessness will pay volunteers $18,000 to lie in bed, there's a catch. (There's always a catch.) "Volunteers spend up to 70 days in bed with a six-degree head-down tilt. They must eat, exercise, and even shower in the head-down position."

Remember puffy-face syndrome, where astronauts' heads swelled because of the zero-gravity environment in space? *Forbes* magazine reports that, during these studies, "researchers study the effects of fluid shifts in participants' bodies, as well as bone and muscle loss often experienced in weightlessness." After the period of prolonged bedrest, "subjects are then put through various exercises, such as going on the treadmill or doing squats. Major difference, though—it's a vertical treadmill, and squatting is done in a horizontal position." Roni Cromwell adds,

"We also ask [test subjects] to do tasks that astronauts would do when they land on a planetary surface. Simulate getting out of a vehicle. Moving heavy objects at a short distance. This gives us an idea as to their functional capabilities."

And while it sounds good, 70 days is a *loooong* time. Participants report that boredom, the controlled diet, and the constant data collection are all challenges. At least family and friends can visit and "hang out" with you when you're there!

DID NASA LOSE THE COMPETITION TO HAVE THE "WRITE" STUFF?

The story goes that in the 1960s, NASA spent gazillions of dollars to develop a pen that could write in microgravity, while their Soviet counterparts, in thrifty wisdom, just used "grease pencils." Well . . . not exactly. NASA historians record that both astronauts

and cosmonauts used pencils at first, but they were expensive, flammable, and could break or flake off and float around the spacecraft, which was dangerous. So in 1965, the Fisher Pen Company patented a pen "that could write upside-down, in frigid or roasting conditions (down to −50°F or up to 400°F), and even underwater or in other liquids. If too hot, though, the ink turned green instead of its normal blue," according to *Scientific American*. The Fisher Pen used pressurized nitrogen to get its gel-like ink flowing. Both the US and the USSR ordered the "anti-gravity" space pens in the late 1960s, and they have been used by astronauts ever since. In fact, it's been reported that it was a space pen that helped save the Apollo 11 mission. From tech blog io9: "In 1969, the AG-7 was onboard when Buzz Aldrin used a pen to activate a broken circuit breaker that helped control the main engines for lifting off the Moon's surface." Fisher space pens are available to the public today.

IS THERE A COLLEGE IN SPACE? DO I NEED TO CALCULATE MY GPA IN LIGHT-YEARS TO APPLY?

As far as we know, there is no college in space. But the International Space University, located in France, offers graduate degrees and "educational programs to students and space professionals in an international, intercultural environment." The ISU seeks to operate as a forum for global cooperation, innovative research, and the study of space for peaceful, cooperative purposes. The current chancellor is Buzz Aldrin, best known as one of NASA's first moonwalkers on the Apollo 11 mission.

ARE THOSE LITTLE GREEN MEN THE REASON WHY WE HAVE AN OFFICE OF PLANETARY PROTECTION?

Uh, not exactly. "The mission of the Office of Planetary Protection is to promote the responsible exploration of the solar system by implementing and developing efforts that protect the science, explored environments, and Earth," says NASA. The office helps NASA conduct its work in a way

that prevents biological contamination of the places we explore and study and that protects the Earth just in case we do one day encounter other intelligent life in the universe. This office works with others at NASA in the development of sterile spacecraft, minimally invasive flight plans, and protective procedures "to protect the Earth from returned extraterrestrial samples." It also develops responsible policies for space exploration and travel. "Ultimately, the objective of planetary protection is to support the scientific study of chemical evolution and the origins of life in the solar system."

DO WE BURY SPACECRAFT IN A SPACE CEMETERY?

Not quite. But there is an area of the Pacific Ocean near New Zealand that is home to about 161 spacecraft that fell from the skies to their watery graves. Officially called the South Pacific Ocean Uninhabited Area, this region is near the point in the ocean that is farthest from land, called Point Nemo—and far from the possibility of landing on or near people. When spacecraft de-orbit, things get pretty messy. They don't just fall in one piece; they burn and break apart. Still, the falls are controlled; ships and aircraft are warned in advance, and debris is generally kept to this uninhabited area.

SHOULD WE RECONSIDER THE US'S DECISION NOT TO GO METRIC?

Well, it might have prevented the loss of a $125 million Mars orbiter back in 1999, after it had already spent almost ten months on its journey to the red planet. Because the two different engineering teams also used two different units of measurement (metric vs. English), information from the spacecraft failed to transfer and commands were scrambled, preventing the spacecraft from getting into orbit around Mars.

"The problem here was not the error; it was the failure of NASA's systems engineering and the checks and balances in our processes to detect the error. That's why we lost the spacecraft," said NASA in a written statement. At the time, CNN reported that "the navigation mishap pushed the spacecraft dangerously close to the planet's atmosphere, where it presumably burned and broke into pieces, killing the mission on a day when engineers had expected to celebrate the craft's entry into Mars's orbit."

DID SCIENTISTS HEAR A SPACE LION ROAR?

Okay, it was not a lion, but they heard . . . *something*. "Space, it turns out, has a background noise," writes Kate Kershner on *How Stuff Works*. That is a little weird, considering that space is a vacuum, so there's no way for sound waves to travel and, well, make noise. But when NASA sent the ARCADE (absolute radiometer for cosmology, astrophysics, and diffuse emission) up, up, and away on a balloon in order to detect and study heat from first-generation stars, "instead of the faint signal we hoped to find, here was this booming noise six times louder than anyone had predicted," says NASA's Alan Kogut, who led the study.

The "roar" came in the form of radio signals, so it wasn't "heard" in the traditional way that we hear sound. But this cosmic noise is big enough to keep us from getting to those earliest stars, and we haven't figured out what exactly it is or where it's coming from. Once we figure it out, we may be able to learn more about the development of galaxies. "This is what makes science so exciting," says NASA's Michael Seiffert. "You start out on a path to measure something—in this case, the heat from the very first stars—but run into something else entirely, something unexplained."

CHAPTER TEN

NASA AND THE ENVIRONMENT

A FORCE FOR POSITIVE CHANGE

TODAY, NASA IS ONE of the entities at the forefront of climate-science research, supporting the work of scientists and researchers around the world in a collaborative effort to understand climate change and find ways to help us care for our planet. NASA does research on rising sea levels, solar activity, the changing temperatures in the oceans and atmosphere, the ozone layer, and the ways that ice has changed over time on land and in the seas.

So . . . how exactly did the agency that was once known only for Moon landings and space wars become a leading partner in understanding the changes in our world, our communities, and our lives right here on Earth?

At the same time that the United States was creating the agency that became NASA, the country was engaging in other activities that would significantly affect our lives on this planet. Scientists believe that since the middle of the twentieth century, human activity has very likely caused much of the Earth's

rapid warming trend. We've been heating ourselves up, literally!

In 1958, when NASA was first established, its focus was "space observation." Other government agencies had the Earth covered, like the Weather Bureau (now National Oceanic and Atmospheric Administration) and the United States Geological Survey. But the environmental movement in the United States had picked up steam with the release of Rachel Carson's 1962 book *The Silent Spring*. Carson's work made many aware of the harmful effects of pesticides on the environment. In 1970, President Nixon founded the Environmental Protection Agency (EPA), responding to increasing concern about the effects that humans were having on the environment. As Congress wondered if NASA could keep its feet a little closer to the ground, NASA Administrator James Fletcher believed strongly in NASA's ability to play a significant role in the world of environmental science. Addressing Congress in 1973, Fletcher declared,

"Everything we do . . . helps in some practical way to improve the environment of our planet and helps us understand the forces that affect it. Perhaps that is our essential task: to study and understand the Earth and its environment."

Apollo 17's iconic *Blue Marble* photo brought a new awareness to Earth's vulnerability. "Our whole planet suddenly, in this image, seemed tiny, vulnerable, and incredibly lonely against the vast blackness of the cosmos," writes neuroscientist Gregory Petsko. "Regional conflict and petty differences could be dismissed as trivial compared with environmental dangers that threatened all of humanity." The *Blue Marble* image became an emblem of the environmental movement. It had an enormous impact on how we thought about our planet, an impact that continues to be felt today.

"The Earth faces environmental problems right now that threaten the imminent destruction of civilization and the end of the planet as a livable world. Humanity cannot afford to waste its financial and emotional resources on endless, meaningless quarrels between each group and all others. There must be a sense of globalism in which the world unites to solve the real problems that face all groups alike."
—Isaac Asimov, science-fiction author and biochemistry professor

THE HOLE IN THE SKY

In 1974, scientists found that *chlorofluorocarbons*—or CFCs, which are gases used in refrigerants, like air conditioners, and in aerosols, like hair spray—were causing damage to the ozone layer in our atmosphere. CFCs had been developed as nonflammable, less-toxic alternatives to refrigerants that had been used since the early part of the twentieth century. Sounds good, right? Well, not so much.

The *ozone layer* is something we kind of want to keep around. It's the layer of the Earth's atmosphere that absorbs harmful ultraviolet (UV) radiation from the sun. Sometimes it's called Earth's "natural sunscreen." Exposure to UV radiation can cause skin cancers and eye disease. It "burns" and damages living tissue if we don't take measures to protect ourselves from it, like by wearing sunscreen and . . . keeping the ozone layer intact. While CFCs might have kept us cool and preserved the kind of helmet hair we wanted in the 1970s, they caused a lot of harm. Scientists conducting research in Antarctica in the 1980s found that ozone levels there were dropping lower than anyone had ever seen. The research showed that, because we were spraying and blowing CFCs into our atmosphere at such a high rate, we were creating a hole in the ozone layer. Businesses that used CFCs in their products didn't like the sound of that and pooh-poohed the idea, but NASA was on the case.

NASA "took one of its high-altitude aircraft and flew into the ozone hole," says NASA Chief Scientist for Earth Sciences Paul Newman. Clouds had been observed in the Antarctic region where there should

stratosphere

ozone

troposphere

not have been conditions to create them; the region is very dry. NASA found high levels of chlorine monoxide in those areas that corresponded to low levels of ozone. It was the chemical reaction of the gases in CFCs with the ozone layer that created those clouds and was contributing to the fast and destructive loss of the protective ozone layer. Newman says that NASA also conducted model simulations that showed that the ozone layer "would be destroyed . . . by 2065. What that means is crops will die and you'd go outside and you would quickly burn." NASA's data helped scientists confirm their hypothesis that CFCs were extremely dangerous to the health of the Earth and its inhabitants, and in September 1987, 56 countries agreed to the Montreal Protocol, an international treaty in which they agreed to work to reduce CFCs in the atmosphere, banning products containing them.

By 1992, all production of substances that destroy the ozone layer had ended. As of 2015, 197 countries around the world were committed to the Montreal Protocol. "Instead of CFCs increasing, CFCs are now going down," says Newman. In 2018, NASA satellite data from Antarctica showed that the decline in chlorine that is a result of the ban on CFCs "has resulted in about 20 percent less ozone depletion during the Antarctic winter than there was in 2005." Woot! Scientists believe that the ozone layer should continue to recover slowly, with our help; CFCs hang around in the atmosphere for a long time—for 50 or even 100 years!—so by 2060 or maybe 2080, the ozone hole could be almost completely closed.

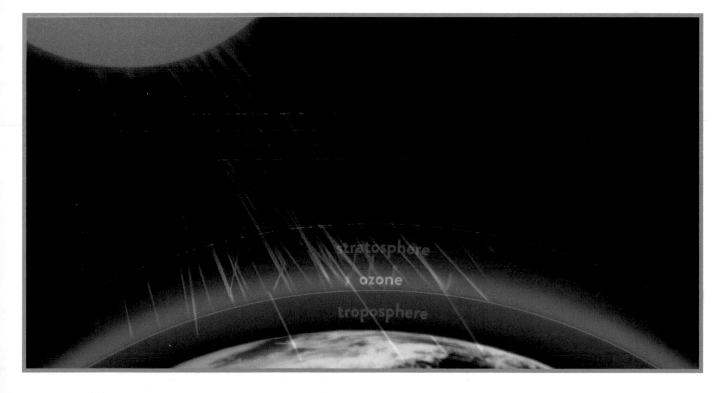

CLIMATE CHANGE AND GLOBAL WARMING
TWO WAYS OF SAYING THE SAME THING?

Nope. *Climate change* is the global phenomena of all the different things that cause heat to become trapped in our atmosphere, which happens as a result of our fossil-fuel burning. Climate change does include the warming temperatures on Earth like global warming, but it also includes rising sea levels, loss of ice, changes in agricultural growing patterns, and extreme-weather events, like hurricanes.

What we do and how we live matters. "The burning of *fossil fuels*—whether it's coal, oil, or natural gas—has released this very, very old carbon back into the atmosphere," says NASA's Peter Griffith, "a lot faster than the oceans and the plants on the land can take it out of the atmosphere." NASA scientists work with others around the world to predict what could happen in the future, creating models of different possibilities.

NASA's ability to collect data about the Earth from space is unique among the US agencies working together on these issues. By the early 1990s, NASA's Earth-observing system was a major part of the world of climate science. NASA started a program called "Global Habitability," now called Mission to Planet Earth (MTPE)—maybe you remember it from Chapter 5! MTPE is "dedicated to understanding the total Earth system and the effects of natural and human-induced changes on the global environment." MTPE research covers climate change and warming caused by greenhouse gases, effects of UV radiation, and more.

Today, NASA has "19 different satellites" studying climate, says Ellen Stofan. Scientists in many different fields are working on these challenges. "They are oceanographers . . . geologists . . . meteorologists . . . NASA's efforts to gather all kinds of geophysical data about this planet brought them together in this new discipline called 'Earth system science,'" says former NASA Chief Historian Roger Launius. Scientists gather data from satellites, aircraft, and teams on the ground. More work has been done to process and analyze that data, so that computer modelers can put together a record of how our planet is changing over time. "We've put together this record over four decades now—a very detailed record—of how the planet is changing," points out Piers Sellers, who was NASA's Acting Director of Earth Sciences.

NASA also collects and analyzes information from other countries' satellites. With over 30 years of satellite-based data, NASA was instrumental in the Intergovernmental Panel on Climate Change's conclusion that "most of the increase in global average temperatures since the mid-twentieth century is very likely due to the observed increase in anthropogenic greenhouse-gas concentrations."

What does that even mean?

NASA measures the ice shelf to see when it has separated and refrozen over time.

"We've seen the ice melting at the North Pole. We've seen the ice melting really fast on Greenland, where it's falling off Greenland into the oceans."
—Piers Sellers, former director of Earth Science at NASA

Our planet's surface temperature has risen about 2°F (1.1° Celsius) since the nineteenth century. But most of the warming has happened very recently. "We've seen this warming over the last century and a half," said Sellers. "Very, very meticulous measurements . . . [show] a really sharp acceleration in the warming over the last four decades."

Some climate change is part of a natural process. Changes in the Earth's orbit or sudden events, like volcanic eruptions, cause cycles of warming and cooling. But scientific research has shown that the rapid changes we're experiencing are due more to the "heat-trapping" gases in our atmosphere than anything else. Those gases—nitrous oxide, methane, and the biggest culprit of all, carbon dioxide—are increasingly in our atmosphere because of *us*, through activities like the burning of fossil fuels and deforestation.

GREENHOUSE GASES

These gases hold heat in our atmosphere—that's why our planet gets warmer. NASA focuses on carbon dioxide. Humans produce more carbon dioxide than any other gas through activity like driving, electricity use, and more.

The *greenhouse effect*: You may hear people use this term when they're talking about climate change. It's the general warming trend of our planet.

Scientific research has found that "the current warming trend is of particular significance" and it's moving at a pace that we've never seen before. Also, as the Earth heats up, more water turns into water vapor in our atmosphere, which heats things up even more, which means more water vapor, which means . . . It's a vicious cycle, but the official name is *positive feedback loop*.

"NASA has given us a global view of Earth, letting us measure what is happening right now on the land surfaces, atmosphere, oceans, and interior of the planet. These global data allow scientists to model how the Earth is changing, study the health of crops and forests, and measure sea-level rise. NASA uses the same instruments to study Earth that it uses to study other planets, allowing us to better understand our own planet by comparing it to other planets like Mars and Venus."

—Ellen Stofan, former chief scientist at NASA

WHAT THE HEAT WAVE MEANS

A degree or two higher in temperature doesn't sound like a big deal, does it? Well, here's what's happened already.

Our oceans are getting warmer. As heat gets trapped in the oceans, ocean chemistry changes. As carbon dioxide is absorbed, the ocean's pH gets lower, making the ocean more acidic—*ocean acidification*. Because of this, coral reefs are "bleached" and the organisms that used to make their habitats there can't survive.

CORAL REEFS

When you bleach fabric, not only does it become whiter, but it also becomes weaker. In fact, it might become so weak that it even disintegrates. This is a little like what happens to coral because of climate change, but coral bleaching has a much more profound impact. Bleached coral is less able to fight disease. Coral depend on *zooxanthellae* (a type of algae) that live in their tissues and provide nutrients—kind of like a food-for-housing exchange. But those algae can't tolerate higher temperatures in warmer oceans, so when it gets too hot, they abandon the coral or sometimes die. Their absence causes coral bleaching. Bleached corals are weakened and unhealthy. If we continue to produce carbon dioxide at the current rate, coral reef skeletons could dissolve and fall apart.

Coral also needs *calcium carbonate* to maintain their skeletons. Ocean acidification depletes the production of calcium carbonate. A more acidic ocean makes it harder for shelled organisms like clams and snails to produce the calcium carbonate they need for their shells.

DOES THE OCEAN NEED AN ANTACID?

Human activity has been releasing more and more carbon dioxide into the atmosphere and, as a result, into our oceans. Scientists have found that ocean acidification has increased by around 30 percent since the late eighteenth century. Some scientists call ocean acidification the "evil twin" of climate change. It's another consequence of too much carbon dioxide in our atmosphere, but its effects are more sharply felt underwater. Because of the warming trend on Earth, so much carbon dioxide is getting absorbed by the oceans that chemicals that used to help maintain a balanced ocean pH can't keep up. And marine life hasn't had a chance to adapt or evolve to keep up, either. Tiny changes in pH can make a big difference. The Smithsonian Museum of Natural History reports that in humans, "normal blood pH ranges between 7.35 and 7.45. A drop in blood pH of 0.2–0.3 can cause seizures, comas, and even death." That tiny difference in pH has a big effect! And it's no different for our oceans. In fact, all of our ecosystems

exist in a delicately balanced and linked world. According to the Smithsonian, "beyond lost biodiversity, acidification will affect fisheries and aquaculture, threatening food security for millions of people, as well as tourism and other sea-related economies." We truly do exist in a "circle of life."

NASA's Coral Reef Airborne Laboratory (CORAL) studies coral all over the world. Research shows that, already, "it is estimated that 33–50 percent of coral reefs worldwide have been largely or completely degraded." CORAL is working to understand all the reasons why we contribute to coral-reef decline. One reason is that surplus nutrients, pollution, and improperly disposed trash get into our soil, which eventually ends up in our oceans. How? Well, as rain falls on land, that water-and-land mix makes its way into our waterways. Whatever is in this sludge—like garbage from our streets and oil from our cars—washes in, too. The water that we swim in, fish from, and drink is affected, and much marine life could die.

"As scientists, we're just taking the most precise data that we can . . . The enormous droughts and fires that we have around the world are directly related to a warmer planet. That has a huge impact on people. It's unprecedented."

—Dava Newman, former deputy administrator at NASA

NASA can't set government policy and decide what we'll do about climate change, but it can and does provide the data we need to help understand what's going on and come up with solutions. "NASA has observed the effects of human-caused climate change on our planet, from rising sea levels, to hurricanes that are wetter and stronger, to changes in vegetation patterns. NASA data is being used to measure the loss of tropical rain forests and the melting of sea ice in the Arctic and ice sheets in Greenland and Western Antarctica," says scientist Stofan. And it's global—NASA's data is available to scientists all over the world.

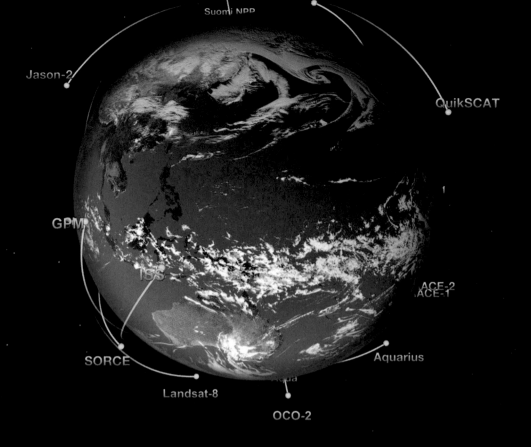

Suomi NPP

Jason-2

QuikSCAT

GPM

ISS

ACE-2
ACE-1

SORCE

Aquarius

Landsat-8

Aqua

OCO-2

WHAT ARE SOME OF THE POSSIBLE EFFECTS OF CLIMATE CHANGE?

THE BAD OLD DAYS: NASA's remote-sensing satellites have found evidence that some ancient civilizations may have declined because of climate change. In the 1980s, NASA used the space shuttle Challenger to take images of ancient desert tracks in the Middle Eastern region now known as Oman. Working with an archeological excavation team, NASA learned that they had discovered the ancient city of Ubar, which was once an important desert outpost and source of water—maybe camels transporting frankincense would gather around this natural "watercooler" and complain about their long workdays. Computer technology even allowed the researchers to see way below the surface sand to traces of the ancient roads that those camels traveled.

NASA's research showed that Ubar was a wet area with abundant underground water sources. Now it's *super*dry. It got so dry that Ubar literally sank out of sight when a sinkhole formed. Other ancient communities seem to have suffered similar fates. What gives? Periods of drought made things unstable—a steady and stable climate meant that communities could (literally) put down roots, grow crops, and build culture. When communities were unable to adjust to changes in climate, they disappeared.

Precipitation (rain, snow, sleet) patterns could continue to change, just like they did for Ubar. Since 1900, average US precipitation has increased, but it's not consistent; some areas have had a big increase while others have had a decline.

Global sea levels are rising, too—there's been a sharp increase in the last two decades, and Arctic sea ice is disappearing. "In the next several decades, storm surges and high tides could combine with sea-level rise and land subsidence to further increase flooding in many regions," reports NASA. "In the Pacific Ocean, islands in the Solomon Islands and Micronesia have been affected, and other island nations such as the Marshall Islands and Kiribati are under threat," says Stofan. "Villages in Kiribati have already been moved to avoid rising sea levels. But even the US is not escaping this—Tangier Island [off the coast of Virginia] is also threatened by rising seas. Sea-level rise will be a global problem, with all countries [that have] low-lying coastal areas affected."

More droughts and heat waves are on the way, too. NASA reports that "by the end of this century, what have been once-in-20-year extreme-heat days (one-day events) are projected to occur every two or three years over most of the nation."

Hurricanes could continue to get stronger, and more destructive: Hurricane strength and frequency has been steadily increasing since the 1980s.

It looks like crazy weather patterns aren't going away anytime soon. "If you have a warmer atmosphere that can hold more moisture . . . that means more convection, more big thunderstorms, more hurricanes, more extreme weather," said Sellers. "That's one of the likely outcomes of a warming world. We've built our civilization around the current climate. Our coastal cities, our food resources, our water resources: They're all pegged to the current climate. And there's not much slack in the system."

Research has already shown us that carbon-dioxide levels in our atmosphere will hang around for years or even generations. So NASA's research suggests that two approaches are needed in response: adaptation and mitigation.

aDaPTaTion anD miTiGaTion

Adaptation means figuring out healthier ways to live in the current climate situation or even using some of the effects of climate change (like longer growing seasons) to our advantage. *Mitigation* is focused on finding ways to reduce the levels of greenhouse gases in the atmosphere and reduce the rate of climate change.

Climate change happens globally, but people around the world are working on local solutions to the problem. Communities are looking at ways to protect themselves from the extreme weather that is caused by climate change, to be more efficient about water use, and to grow crops that can handle our rapidly changing climate.

NASA's Megacities Carbon Project works to measure and monitor greenhouse-gas emissions from the world's big cities. Two percent of the Earth's land surfaces emits about three-fourths of the carbon dioxide in the world! NASA's research will help cities develop systems to monitor and reduce these emissions.

"NASA is . . . taking what we've learned about our planet from space and creating new products that help us all safeguard our future."
—Ellen Stofan, former chief scientist at NASA

One of NASA's best tools for studying environmental conditions on Earth is an oldie but a definite goodie: Landsat. Landsat's remote-sensing satellites, in operation for more than four decades, have been collecting a ginormous amount of data about the Earth's land surfaces. Every 99 minutes, a Landsat satellite makes an orbit around the Earth, and by the time 16 days are up, Landsat satellites have covered the entire globe. Fancier tools have been developed since Landsat came on the scene in 1972, but none of them have the long record of data, easy access, and cost-effectiveness of Landsat.

DID YOU KNOW?

Landsat Island is a tiny island located off the coast of Canada. It was discovered by the Landsat satellite in 1976—hence the name! Landsat Island's existence was verified by Frank Hall, a task that, according to NASA, was a little more challenging than expected:

Hall "was strapped into a harness and lowered from a helicopter down to the island," reports NASA. This was quite a frozen island, and it was completely covered with ice. As he was lowered out of the helicopter, a polar bear took a swat at him. The bear was on the highest point on the island, and it was hard for [Hall] to see because it was white. Hall yanked at the cable and got himself hauled up. He said he very nearly became the first person to end his life on Landsat Island."

Landsat photo of Earth's surface.

What does *remote sensing* even mean? Did you know that *you* are a remote sensor? Don't worry— you're still human. See, *remote sensing* means collecting information about an object without touching it. So if you see and hear a lion roar, you've got some data (and probably should get out of its way!). Remote sensors can be cameras attached to trucks and planes here on Earth or on satellites in space.

ICESat

NASA scientists spend a lot of time measuring and analyzing ice thickness in polar regions. Why? Data shows us that in our warming oceans, glaciers are retreating all over the world. The Ice, Clouds, and Land Elevation Satellite (ICESat) examines ice thickness and other geographic information from arctic ice sheets. "ICESat and its team of talented scientists and engineers helped us see the Earth's polar ice caps in a new way. Those observations are feeding a new generation of models to help us figure out where the planet is headed," said NASA's Tom Wagner. ICESat showed that Arctic sea ice is rapidly getting thinner, and that Greenland is losing ice, which is contributing to rising sea levels. Launched in 2003, ICESat's mission ended in 2010, when it shut down. It remains in space, and will eventually re-enter the Earth's atmosphere—but most of the spacecraft will burn up before it reaches Earth's surface. ICESat-2 is scheduled to launch in 2018.

ICEBRIDGE

Until ICESat-2 gets going, IceBridge is doing important work to collect detailed data from the Earth's polar ice in the Arctic and Antarctic regions—data that can be used to better understand the regions' response to climate change and the rising sea levels that accompany it. Research aircraft carrying science instruments fly over the regions annually, conducting the largest airborne survey of polar ice ever.

Our most vulnerable communities are often the first to be affected by climate change that can increase the risks of poverty, food insecurity, and unsafe water supplies. Ellen Stofan points out that "what we see is a planet that is changing very rapidly due to the actions of humans, in a way that is a threat to all life on Earth." Sellers said, "NASA has an immense capability to really study these changes—how much fossil fuel we burn, how much carbon dioxide we release into the atmosphere." He continued, "The kind of climate we're going to get depends entirely on us humans and what we decide to do."

"When we look outward, when we understand the planets, when we go out into the universe, we're really still trying to look back at ourselves and say, 'How does our planet work?'"
—Ellen Stofan, former chief scientist at NASA

CITIZEN SCIENTIST: HOW YOU CAN HELP

"Young people are really smart and understand climate and the world around them," says Dava Newman, former deputy administrator at NASA. "They can talk to their friends, schoolmates, and parents about our changing climate . . . They can act. Young people are great advocates for the oceans, land and air, nature, and species both on land and in our oceans. They can be examples, especially for their families and friends, by acting to help regenerate. Examples might be: asking to take public transportation rather than having their parents drive them, using recycled materials, and recycling everything they can. They can also reduce their carbon footprint by eating healthy vegetable food choices [instead of] eating meat."

LEARN MORE about the climate and Earth's systems: Earth.nasa.gov

GET INVOLVED with NASA's GLOBE program, where you can contribute climate measurements: Globe.gov/

MAKE AND DO real engineering and science projects that help NASA's work: NASA.gov/solve/index

USE LESS WATER. While long, hot showers might feel good for a little while, they are wasteful. As the Earth's population grows, more people will need clean water, which is a precious-but-not-unlimited resource. Many regions of the world are experiencing drought. Here in the US, residents of the city of Flint, Michigan, have been instructed to use bottled water because high levels of lead were found in Flint's water supply in 2014. Turning off the water while you're brushing your teeth, fixing a running or leaky toilet, and using water stored in buckets instead of from a running hose can all save significant amounts of water.

REDUCE, REUSE, RECYCLE. Paper, aluminum cans, glass, and plastic are all recyclable. Computers and electronics are, too! Find out when your community collects recycled items, or work with local officials to set up a recycling program. Use a refillable water bottle if you have access to clean water. Use reusable steel straws instead of single-use plastic ones. Ask your family to collect and use reusable shopping bags at the grocery store—plastic grocery bags are *not* easily recyclable.

LIMIT CAR USE. Walk, ride your bike, or use public transportation to reduce carbon emissions. Try carpooling whenever you do have to use a car.

These are just a few ways that you can work to preserve our planet and have an impact on climate change and global warming in our world. NASA's Student Guide to Global Climate Change (www3.epa.gov/climatechange//kids) offers real world opportunities for anyone to get involved in collecting

Astronaut and physicist Sally Ride, who became the first US woman in space in 1983, died in 2012, but her legacy continues to inspire. In 1995 she created an educational outreach program that put a camera on space shuttles so that students around the world can access images of specific places on Earth from the unique vantage point of space. Today, the Sally Ride EarthKAM camera is on the ISS, and during its missions (which happen about four times a year), it takes pictures of places at the request of participating schools. Along with images, archived photos are available online, and the program offers resources and activities to engage young people in "Earth and space science, geography, social studies, mathematics, communications, and art." To go on a mission, visitEarthKAM.org.

data that helps scientists understand the changes in our climate and their effects. Observe migrating birds and butterflies, collect information about coral reefs, track plant and flower growth, and more.

NASA "is a space agency, a science and technology agency, and an environmental agency," writes Professor W. Henry Lambert, the author of several books about NASA's history. "It does not make environmental policy, but its activities provide new scientific knowledge that impacts environmental values and . . . political debate over policy." NASA's work of interplanetary exploration has provided us with information that can help shape our thinking and decision-making about our own environment right here on Earth. NASA technology, particularly its satellites, has been instrumental in collecting the data we need to understand what's happening on our planet. But some wonder if NASA is also contributing to some of the less-positive changes in our environment. Does "space junk" contaminate space? Do our spacecraft bring unfamiliar bacteria and germs to other planets? Do the materials used to build our technology do harm? As NASA moves forward and continues its work to ensure our planet's health, many believe that it must also look to answering these questions as well.

Piers Sellers, who contributed to the development of the ISS and made three trips to the ISS space laboratory, also worked on the development of NASA's Terra satellite, which was built to measure and monitor climate change. "I've been fortunate enough to see the Earth from space, when I was an astronaut," said Sellers in his last video message before his death in 2016. "We all live on an unbelievably beautiful planet . . . I've spent most of my life trying to better understand how the Earth system works. The science community . . . is firmly convinced that we humans are changing the planet, and the climate, in a potentially disastrous way. To make the changes we need to make, and to reach a safer future, we will need the resources of everybody . . . all working together toward a common goal. And that goal is a planet that can continue to support life. Including all of us."

HELIX NEBULA
700 LIGHT-YEARS

CHAPTER ELEVEN
NEW VISIONS, NEW VOICES

"We know that creative minds and innovators do not all come in the same package—they don't look alike, think alike, or come from the same regional, educational, or cultural backgrounds. Those are facts—and we must continue to take them into account if we want to go on arriving at the best technical solutions and building on NASA's legacy as a world leader in science, aeronautics, space exploration, and technology."

—Charles Bolden, former NASA administrator

IN A 2016 REQUEST for proposals, NASA directly addressed the issues of diversity and inclusion. "NASA recognizes and supports the benefits of having diverse and inclusive" communities and "fully expects that such values will be reflected in the composition of all proposal teams." NASA scientists hope that language like this will encourage people from all walks of life to consider working with the agency. Young people like Taylor Richardson, also known as "Astronaut StarBright," are embracing the idea that the world of space and space travel is for them, and they're spreading the word.

Mae Jemison's book, *Find Where the Wind Goes*, sparked Taylor's interest in space travel when she was in third grade. She went to Space Camp in Huntsville, Alabama, and her dream blossomed. "I always wanted to be different when I was little, so since no one has been to Mars, I always wanted to go," said Taylor in an interview with NBC. Taylor wants to be the first African American on Mars. The future astronaut has given herself a mission here on Earth as well: to promote the love of literacy and STEM in children across the country. She's a MARS Generation Student Ambassador, one of a group of youth advocates and activists who share their love of space exploration and work to create change in their own communities.

In 2015, as a middle schooler, Taylor created a book drive called "Taylor's Take Flight with a Book."

In partnership with the United Way ReadingPals program, she did space-themed read-alouds (dressed in her astronaut suit!) and collected more than 500 new and gently used books, which were later distributed to local children. "I feel every kid deserves a book," says Taylor on the MARS Generation site. "Books can take you to great places, and those places can lead to great possibilities." By 2017, she had read to over 250 children and collected more than 3,500 books.

After seeing a White House screening of the film *Hidden Figures* in 2016, Taylor was inspired and wanted to give other children the same opportunity. So she started a GoFundMe campaign that raised almost $20,000. The campaign's goals were to host screenings and offer free tickets to the film, as well as a copy of the book that inspired the film to more than 800 children in her hometown of Jacksonville, Florida—and beyond! She also sponsored a scholarship so that another girl would have the opportunity to attend Space Camp.

Along with her activism, Taylor continues to prepare for a future in space. "I love everything about space," she told *Women You Should Know*. "Space is everything—not just other galaxies and far-off planets . . . Space is the tree I climb as a kid, space is every piece of art you've ever seen, and space is everything that happens in the universe, including our little planet. Knowing that, not liking space would be crazy to me."

Experiences with childhood bullying also led Taylor to start anti-bullying campaigns. Diagnosed with ADHD, which she describes as "Abundantly Different, Happily Divine," the honor student also trains by learning other languages, like Spanish and Chinese, and competing in triathlons. She plans to become the first black girl to visit all NASA Space Centers before she graduates from high school. Taylor is the recipient of many awards and honors and got to meet her inspiration, Mae Jemison, in 2016. "Seeing her makes me feel like I can do anything as long as I put my mind to it. Having someone like Dr. Jemison, who looks like me, makes me feel good about myself . . . She's not just an African American role model, she's a role model for all people and girls like me who want to live their dreams of becoming astronauts."

Newman says, "I change the STEM conversation to . . . STEAMD—science, technology, engineering, art, math, and design. If kids are passionate about art, they are visionaries and storytellers, and NASA needs them for future missions to send people to Mars and back or to discover life elsewhere in the universe; to paint the pictures and tell the stories of exploration. If kids are designers or makers and love 3-D printing or Legos, then NASA needs them for their creativity and hands-on problem solving. NASA also has many engineers, scientists, and mathematicians. The most important mind-set is always remaining curious and asking questions to learn more. Also making sure to believe in the beauty of your dreams . . . Being a rocket scientist is my favorite job in the world!"

ASTRONAUT ABBY

Abigail "Abby" Harrison has been telling the world about her dream to be the first person to set foot on Mars since she was 13 years old, and at 20 years old, she is well on her way to making that happen. As a public-school student in Saint Paul, Minnesota, Abby spent extra time on STEM education projects and programs, joining in the Science Bowl team and in Girls in Engineering Math and Science, and made time for gymnastics, track and field, Model UN, and advanced math, science, and engineering classes. Currently a student at Wellesley College, where she's studying astrobiology and Russian, "Astronaut Abby" also founded an internationally recognized nonprofit, the Mars Generation, when she was only 18 years old!

The mission of her award-winning organization is to "excite young people and adults about human space exploration and STEM/STEAMD education and foster an understanding of the importance of these two elements to the future of humankind on Earth." The Mars Generation conducts outreach programs, offers Space Camp scholarships, and nurtures future astronauts through a mentorship program called the Student Space Ambassador Program. "What I have learned is that people have so much power to help shape the destiny of others, simply by offering a helping hand," says Abby. Astronaut Abby is an active social media user and hosts a weekly #AskAbby space and science show on YouTube. On the show, she asks and answers viewer questions, from "Should we bring puppies with us to Mars?" (Answer: "Hmmmm . . . maybe not in their best interests.") to "Can astronauts experience motion sickness in space?" (Answer: "Yeah, kind of . . . it's called space adaptation syndrome.")

Astronaut Abby has conducted biology research in Russia, completed an internship at the Kennedy Space Center, and worked with her mentor, Italian astronaut Luca Parmitano, to share stories and information about an astronaut's life and work. She met Parmitano when she had the opportunity to attend the final launch of the space shuttle Endeavor. Parmitano told her, "Follow your heart in your studies, and do what you love. NASA is looking for people who are passionate about what they do." Astronaut Abby is definitely passionate about the mission to Mars—she believes it's vital to our survival. "For the sake of the future of humanity here on Earth, we must put humanity elsewhere. We must send humans to Mars . . . Mars is a challenging journey, which will push our understanding of our solar system, our knowledge of what we are capable of accomplishing, and our scientific and technological abilities," she says. "Mars is just difficult enough to provide us with the challenge humans need to keep pushing ourselves to innovate and advance our own abilities on Earth."

Even NASA's professional scientists must continue to challenge themselves, says Stofan. "I worked with a team of scientists and engineers to design a possible future mission to one of Saturn's moons, called Titan. Titan has seas of *liquid hydrocarbons*—basically gasoline—because it is very, very cold so far from the Sun. We designed a floating probe for half the cost that others had estimated by really pushing the technology and science. The mission has not been selected to fly yet, but it shows what is possible when you are innovative."

And diversity goes hand in hand with innovation. New voices bring new ideas and new possibilities. In 2018, NASA hosted Vishavjit "Vish" Singh, a "software engineer–turned-cartoonist-turned-superhero" who's nicknamed the "Sikh Captain America." Singh is an advocate for diversity in the workplace. "The research now shows the best teams are those that take advantage of the diverse skills, knowledge, and viewpoints that are available," says NASA Program Scientist Curt Niebur.

Homero Palaguachi would probably agree. Homero aspires to be the first autistic astronaut, and during a visit to NASA's Langley Research Center, he said, "I want to bring a message to other kids who have disabilities: that they can achieve their potential." During his junior year of high school, Homero's math skills, determination, and positive attitude so impressed his teacher, Chris Canik, that Canik organized a fundraiser to send Homero on that visit to NASA. In a letter to NASA, Canik wrote, "[Homero] holds his own despite every struggle, every opportunity for failure, and every understandable excuse a lesser man might make . . . Homero is a hero in our school to both myself and to the many students he calls friends." The visit was successfully funded for Homero *and* 14 of his classmates, and they got to tour the Langley facilities and meet astronaut Charles Camarda. Camarda gave Homero a signed photo inscribed with the words *Reach for the stars, and never give up.* And he hasn't. "The more well-rounded and resourceful I get," says Homero, "the chances are limitless."

HOW TO: ACHIEVING SPACE DREAMS

How do ordinary kids get to do these extraordinary things? When Astronaut Abby was only 14, she was blogging for NASA and taking extra courses in science and math to prepare for reaching her astronaut goals. Taylor Richardson has said that she plans to major in engineering and African American studies in college. Kids who dream of being a part of NASA get this advice from the agency itself: "To 'get to NASA' as a teenager? Or to be a guest blogger at NASA? *How do you do that?* The answer is this: You love learning; you find a passion and set goals; and you work to make those goals happen." NASA advises that future astronauts, engineers, and anyone interested in the study of our world and beyond should "challenge yourself to reach further and to push yourself beyond what you're used to." Jessica Watson, a member of NASA's 2017 astronaut class, started out studying engineering but developed a passion for geology, and works on the Mars Curiosity Rover project. The process of becoming an astronaut, she says, "is so rigorous and the statistics are so small, you want to pursue something that you really love and that you would love to do for the rest of your life."

Thinking in new ways and risking failure are also part of the world of science. NASA is all about innovation, and innovation involves a little bravery. Dr. Ayanna Howard, who works at NASA on developing robots for future Mars missions, points out that "it takes insane courage to innovate. Courage to open yourself up for criticism. To be in a place where no one has the same diverse experience as you—and be confident that your difference is what makes your ability to innovate unique."

NASA has worked with the 4-H organization to develop a set of team-building, leadership, collaboration, and communication activities that can help kids develop the skills they need to become astronauts—or work in any field. (https://www.nasa.gov/audience/foreducators/stem-on-station/expeditionary-skills-for-life.html)

"We need to make sure we are encouraging all kids to become scientists and engineers—and help change the world. I struggled sometimes in my math and science courses, so I also think it is important for kids to know you don't have to be the best in science and math to grow up to have an amazing career in science. Research shows that diverse teams perform better and get better results. We don't know who the person is who is going to help us get to Mars or help solve the problems caused by climate change, so we need to make sure we are not excluding anyone."

—Ellen Stofan, former chief scientist at NASA

PROFILE: SUNITA WILLIAMS

In 2007, Boston Marathon runners ran in 48°F weather conditions, with a little misty rain and 28-mile-per-hour winds. One runner—number 14,000—ran with them, though her conditions were a little different. For her, it was 78°F, with no wind or rain . . . and she was in space. Astronaut Sunita Williams ran the Boston Marathon while working as a flight engineer on the International Space Station. Williams, who wanted to encourage young people to engage in physical fitness, had to be harnessed to a special treadmill by bungee cords in order to run. "I thought a big goal like a marathon would help get this message out there," she said.

Williams completed the marathon in a time of 4 hours, 23 minutes, and 10 seconds. In that time, she circled the Earth at least twice, "running as fast as eight miles per hour but flying more than five miles each second," according to NASA. Not a surprise for the astronaut who held longtime spacewalking records (a total of seven, which was the most by a woman until Peggy Whitson, in 2017). "When you're on a spacewalk, it's just you out there in your space suit, so you get a nice 360-degree view of the whole Earth and the universe," Williams told students in a live conversation from the ISS. "It's really spectacular."

Williams started out wanting to be a veterinarian, then ended up joining the navy and becoming a pilot. She's been a diving officer and helicopter pilot and was in charge of a Hurricane Andrew relief mission. She believes that these experiences helped her develop the leadership and teamwork skills needed to be a successful astronaut. She was a member of NASA's NEEMO 2 crew, where she lived underwater in NASA's Aquarius habitat in Florida for nine days.

In addition to serving as a flight engineer during her time on the ISS, WIlliams also served as commander for Expedition 33. In two missions on the ISS, Williams spent a total of 322 days in space. "When you are thinking about going away for a long-duration mission, it has to be part of your mind-set that you're leaving your family, but it's for the right reasons, for good reasons and hopefully helping humanity," she told the BBC. "You want to make sure that when you leave, you feel at peace with everything." Williams decided to donate her hair to charity, and while she was on the ISS, fellow astronaut and engineer Joan E. Higginbotham, who worked with Williams to operate the ISS robot arm, gave her ponytail the big space chop. The ponytail was donated to the organization Locks of Love—their first donation from an astronaut in space.

Williams, who is the second astronaut of Indian descent to travel into space (her friend Kalpana Chawla was first), brought the sacred Hindu texts, the Bhagavad Gita and the Upanishads, with her, along with some samosas and some Slovenian sausages (her mother is Slovenian American). Williams made "fluffernutters" on the ISS—with peanut butter and marshmallow creme on tortillas—and even "hacked" a tuna casserole by mixing a packet of tuna with rehydrated macaroni and cheese. When she asked NASA to spice up the food supply, a tube of wasabi sent up to the ISS accidentally squirted out into the weightless environment and ended up all over the place. Normally, "it's always fun to throw your food around up here, because it really doesn't fall—you just catch it," Williams told students. But flying wasabi was a bit of a challenge. "We finally got the wasabi smell out after it was flying around everywhere . . . We cleaned it up off the walls a little bit," Williams reported to her mom in a call. Williams suffered another mishap when her camera came undone during a seven-hour spacewalk and floated away. (Other items that have escaped into space include Ed White's glove during Gemini 4; Michael Collins's camera, which came along for the ride on Gemini 10; and a thermal blanket from STS-88.)

In September 2012, Williams became the first person to complete a triathlon in space, using the ISS treadmill and stationary bike for the running and biking portions. How did she swim? Williams used the spacecraft's advanced resistive exercise device (ARED) to do weightlifting and resistance exercises that were similar to the effort required to swim in microgravity. Her finish time was reported as 1 hour, 48 minutes, and 33 seconds. "Don't get bogged down by the notion of limits," she said in an interview with the *Wall Street Journal*. "There aren't any."

PROFILE: JOHN BENNETT HERRINGTON

The launch of a space shuttle is always historic, but the 2002 Endeavor also carried the first enrolled member of a Native American nation to space. John Bennett Herrington—a Chickasaw man, navy veteran, and Oklahoma native—was a mission specialist on STS-113, the sixteenth space shuttle mission to the ISS. He points out that, though he didn't have visible role models in his astronaut training, his heritage offers an important perspective on the study of space. "Long before there was western science, our ancestors were doing remarkable things in observing the world around us and making structures that captured the solar cycle . . . Native people have been very talented engineers and scientists for millennia," Herrington said in an interview with *Indian Country*. "They did it for survival. You have to be very observant to the world around you in order to survive." On his space shuttle mission, Herrington brought symbols of his heritage and Nation, including a flute, an eagle feather, arrowheads, and sweet grass. He also carried the flag of the Chickasaw Nation.

Herrington's college career had a slightly rocky start. He loved the mountains and outdoors and spent "lots of time climbing and too little time studying." Because of low grades, he was suspended from the University of Colorado. But after a break, he decided to go back to school and went on to earn a master's degree in aeronautical engineering, then become a navy test pilot and a NASA astronaut. And it turns out that old rock-climbing experience may have come in handy. Newspaper *The Spokesman-Review* reports: "On his final spacewalk, he was forced to improvise a way of attaching small devices all over the station to correct a design flaw in the ammonia line connections. Plans called for him to be held in place by a robot arm, but the arm became stuck. So he found himself faced with the task one-handed—which would have been tricky in normal gravity, let alone floating above the Earth wearing a glove like an oven mitt."

After retiring from NASA, Herrington spent three months biking across the country, from Cape Flattery, Washington, to Cape Canaveral, Florida. He took this 2008 "Rocketrek" to encourage Native children to get involved with his passions: science and math. On the trip, he discovered another passion when he met his wife, author Margo Aragon. The two went on to create a company: Herrington Aerospace Limited. Herrington also wrote a children's book called *Mission to Space* that includes a Chickasaw-English space vocabulary list.

In 2011, Herrington went back to school again—this time for a PhD in education, which he received in 2014. "I like to solve problems. I like to see how stuff works. I like challenges. My ancestors were able to rise to challenges that came their way. I'd like to say I'm doing the same thing." He studied strategies that got Shoshone-Paiute children involved in science programs like NASA's Summer of Innovation. Part of his research involved creating a battery for classroom use that was powered by . . . poop. "Kids like space," Herrington says. "Kids like dinosaurs. And, for whatever reason, fecal matter's interesting [to them] . . . If you catch their attention, they're going to start asking why."

Infinite Diversity in Infinite Combinations
—Vulcan Philosophy, *Star Trek*

In 2001, groundbreaking astronaut Sally Ride and her partner Tam O'Shaughnessy started Sally Ride Science, a nonprofit that continues to promote the engagement of girls and underrepresented minorities in STEM activities and education. In 2010, NASA cryogenic technician Amy Weston expressed hope of being the first openly transgender astronaut. Today, NASA includes an Out and Allied at NASA resource group at the Johnson Space Center; the group created an "It Gets Better" video in support of LGBTQ youth in 2013. "Teamwork is one of our greatest assets," says Director Ellen Ochoa in the video. "And that means we value the skills and talents of every individual, regardless of differences, including sexual orientation or gender identity." SCIVIS, Space Camp for Interested Visually Impaired Students, is an accessible weeklong camp program in Huntsville, Alabama, that offers kids with disabilities opportunities to "reach for the stars."

In an interview with *TIME* magazine, NASA's first Latino astronaut, Franklin Chang Díaz, describes "the handful of powerful countries most invested in space as 'a little bit of a club' that is 'growing too slowly.'"

He expressed hope that space exploration would be open to all as we move forward. Dava Newman adds, "More diversity means excellence! Plain and simple, more-diverse workforces are excellent and outperform less-diverse workforces. Excellence = Diversity and Inclusion, and that's how we can improve NASA, through diversity and inclusion to bring about more excellence in our work and missions."

"NASA continues to work hard to diversify our workforce and help to inspire the leaders of tomorrow," wrote Newman in 2016. "We have to take bold steps to ensure that we significantly increase the number of women and people of color in NASA's STEM workforce, because we need their perspectives and excellence . . . If we are looking to truly be more inclusive, we need to invite participation by all, including those who may not see themselves as scientists and engineers, but who connect with the arts, design, and the maker movement . . . Through expanding who we reach out to, who we recruit, and also how we are teaching—by changing the conversation to filter everyone 'in' rather than filtering anyone 'out'—we can truly make a difference in creating not just more diverse student populations in STEM but more excellence in our professional work environments."

PROFILE: JONNY KIM

When Jonny Kim found out that he was accepted into NASA's 2017 class of astronaut candidates, he was grocery shopping—and working as an ER doctor. Space travel might have seemed like an unexpected detour for this formerly shy child who struggled in school, but Kim has experience taking a nontraditional path. When he was about to graduate from high school, "I didn't like the person I was growing up to become," he said in an interview with the *Harvard Gazette*. "I needed to find myself and my identity. And for me, getting out of my comfort zone, getting away from the people I grew up with, and finding adventure—that was my odyssey, and it was the best decision I ever made."

Getting out of his comfort zone meant becoming a Navy SEAL and earning Silver and Bronze Stars. His military experience was extremely challenging, and Kim has described wanting to quit at times. But he persevered and served as a combat medic, sniper, navigator, and more on over 100 combat operations in the Middle East. The realities of combat hit hard. "I don't watch a lot of war films and documentaries anymore," he said. "Losing a lot of good friends galvanized me and made a lot of my remaining teammates make sure we made our lives worthwhile. I still, to this day, every day, think of all the good people who didn't get a chance to come home. I try to make up for the lives and positive [impact] they would have had if they were alive."

Kim, third from left, with his 2017 NASA Astronaut Class at the Johnson Space Center.

After his military service, Kim found another calling in medicine. "In emergency medicine, what I appreciated was being able to help people in a critical hour of need . . . having that profound effect of saving someone's life." Selected from a record 18,300 applicants, Kim became one of 12 to undergo the two-year training program. Kim believes that his medical training will be particularly helpful in space. "Medicine is great in that it is a field of undifferentiated data that you have to sort through to make a diagnosis and then a treatment plan," he said in an interview. "I think that helps in a career in space, where you also have undifferentiated data [and] you don't know what the situation is going to hold for you in the future, but you leverage the strengths and weaknesses of yourself and your team members to get through the problem set and reach a good outcome. I think it's not just medicine that has these skill sets; other fields in STEM have the same principles of working through problems with limited data . . . to reach a conclusion."

CRAB NEBULA
6500 LIGHT-YEARS

CHAPTER TWELVE

LIVING IN SPACE, JOURNEY TO MARS . . . AND BEYOND

NASA STARTED the twenty-first century with its plans in trouble again. In November 2001, the George W. Bush administration put the International Space Station program on probation, and the space shuttle Columbia tragedy in 2003 appeared to be a sign to many that our days of putting humans in space should come to an end. Still, as he memorialized the Columbia crew, President Bush said, "The cause of exploration and discovery is not an option we choose; it is a desire written in the human heart. We are that part of creation which seeks to understand all creation. We find the best among us, send them forth into unmapped darkness, and pray they will return. They go in peace for all mankind, and all mankind is in their debt." The following year, President Bush announced his Constellation Program, one

that would broaden the "human presence across the solar system, starting with a human return to the Moon by the year 2020, in preparation for human exploration of Mars and other destinations," and that the space shuttle would no longer be launched after 2010, when the ISS was scheduled to be completed. A new spacecraft would be developed to carry humans to the Moon and beyond.

The Obama administration, historic in many ways, continued to make history when it came to NASA. Charles F. Bolden was appointed as NASA administrator—the first African American to hold the post. The administration also canceled the Constellation Program, saying that it was far behind schedule and way over budget; the US was not quite ready to get people back on the Moon by 2020. The Orion capsule, originally developed as a vehicle for flights to the ISS and the Moon, became a sort of space ambulance—an emergency-escape vehicle for the ISS. President Obama asked NASA to work on getting astronauts to an asteroid by 2025, then the Moon in the 2030s. NASA began developing new technology, including the Asteroid Redirect Mission (ARM), which would grab a giant space rock off an asteroid and then bring it to the Moon's orbit, where astronauts could study it.

President Obama extended the life of the ISS, which was not guaranteed to be in orbit beyond 2015. And one day we may be hailing space cabs—commercial spaceflight also came closer to being reality. Two private companies, SpaceX and Boeing, now provide vehicles that act as taxis, carrying astronauts to the ISS. NASA got its Commercial Orbital Transportation Services program going in 2006, bringing us closer to the idea of ordinary people boldly going where only a few have gone before. Jeff Bezos, CEO of online retail giant Amazon, created the private space company Blue Origin. Bezos claims the company is almost ready to take customers to suborbital space (and back). Virgin Galactic (of airline Virgin Atlantic fame) says the same.

STARMAN AND THE FALCON

On February 6, 2018, the stuff of science fiction really seemed possible. Billionaire Elon Musk launched Falcon Heavy from Kennedy Space Center. This mega powerful rocket was developed by Musk's SpaceX company to carry humans beyond Earth's orbit, to the Moon, Mars, and maybe even to asteroids. It carried one of Musk's cars, a Tesla Roadster, as its payload. "Driving" the car was Starman, a mannequin dressed like an astronaut. The words DON'T PANIC! were on the dashboard, and Musk said that the song "Space Oddity" by David Bowie blared from the speakers. Earth viewers watched a live webcast of the launch, observing Starman spin in space. After reaching Earth's orbit, the Falcon was in "cruise control" for a few hours, meandering through space, then it launched Starman and the Tesla out into deep space. On March 20, 2018, the site Where Is Roadster? calculated that they were over 100 million miles from Mars and moving at a speed of more than 37,000 miles per hour. They're out there, somewhere, not panicking.

Some were unhappy with the cancellation of Constellation and the apparent withering of the dream of traveling to Mars. But Apollo 11 astronaut Buzz Aldrin seemed to like the administration's plans:

"I continue to be excited about the development of commercial capabilities to send humans into low-Earth orbit and what this could ultimately mean in terms of allowing others to experience the transformative power of spaceflight," said Aldrin in a statement. "I can personally attest to what such an experience can do in creating a different perspective regarding our life on Earth and on our future. I applaud the president for his boldness and commitment in working to make this worthwhile dream a reality."

While the Obama administration appeared to have kept the purse strings somewhat tight on planetary exploration, it did continue to prioritize the Earth science capabilities that NASA has become known for. "Government agencies, scientists, private entities, and other stakeholders rely on NASA to process raw information received from Earth-observation systems into useable data," stated a report by NASA's inspector general. "Moreover, NASA's Earth-observation data is routinely used by government agencies, policymakers, and researchers to expand understanding of the Earth system and to enhance economic competitiveness, protect life and property, and develop policies to help protect the planet."

"Because NASA's part of the executive branch [of government], it gets its direction from the president, but then Congress ultimately decides on NASA's budget," said Stofan in an interview on Neil deGrasse Tyson's radio show, *StarTalk*. "If you look back over the history of NASA, [then] at the time of Apollo, NASA was about 4 percent of the federal budget . . . right now NASA's about 0.4 percent . . . So you have to make choices." Even with budget constraints, "NASA's doing a lot of amazing things, and those things actually benefit us every day."

BILLIONS AND BILLIONS OF . . . *PLANETS?*

"The ways by which men arrive at knowledge of the celestial things are hardly less wonderful than the nature of these things themselves." —Johannes Kepler, astronomer

We have seventeenth-century German astronomer Johannes Kepler to thank for furthering our understanding of telescopes. The first to explain how telescopes work, Kepler clarified a lot, including how tides are affected by the Moon, how depth perception works, and what planetary motion is. Kepler's third law, published in 1619, led Isaac Newton to his discovery and understanding of gravity. Put very simply, the law states that the farther a planet is from the Sun, then the slower it moves in its orbit.

The Kepler Space Observatory was launched in 2009 and has been on the hunt for

Locations of planets from other universes found by the Kepler space telescope planets outside of our solar system ever since. To date, thousands of these *exoplanets* have been discovered by the space-based telescope. "As of March 2018, Kepler had found 2,342 confirmed planets; add potential planets, and its find of *exoworlds* stands at 4,587," reports Space.com. Though it was reported in March 2018 that Kepler may soon run out of fuel, it's done some amazing work already, including the 2011 discovery of Kepler 22b, an exoplanet that orbits within the *habitable zone*—or livable area—of a Sun-like star. This means its orbit is close enough (and far enough) to its "sun" to support liquid water, and ultimately life. This made it "the most Earth-like planet we've yet discovered." Astronomers have suggested that there are at least 17 billion Earth-size planets in our galaxy. Is there life on these planets? Time (with the help of technological tools like Kepler) will tell.

"Kepler," reports NASA, "offers astronomers the rare opportunity to monitor single patches of sky continuously for months, like a car's dashboard camera that is always recording."

In addition to planets, Kepler has been useful in the discovery of other space phenomena, like exploding stars, or *supernovae*. "Kepler opened up a new way of looking at the sky," says Jessie Dotson, Kepler's project scientist at NASA. "It was designed to do one thing really well, which is to find planets around other stars. In order to do that, it had to deliver high-precision, continuous data, which has been valuable for other areas of astronomy." Kepler can help scientists see how and why stars explode and can help them observe the process over time. Understanding supernovae will help scientists understand the universe's expansion.

"NASA is looking for life beyond Earth, from the surface of Mars to beneath the icy crusts of Jupiter's moon Europa and Saturn's moon Enceladus," says Stofan. "Scientists are optimistic that we will find evidence that life evolved beyond Earth in our own solar system. At the same time, NASA has found over 2,500 planets around other stars. We are searching for an Earth-like planet that could possibly host life. We really are on the verge of answering the age-old question of [whether we are] alone in the universe!"

CREAKY BONES, FALLING FINGERNAILS . . . ASTRONAUTS OR SPACE ZOMBIES?

"Living in zero-G is the equivalent of a long stay in a hospital . . . You lose muscle mass and strength. You lose blood volume. You lose aerobic fitness, anaerobic fitness, stamina . . . Spaceflight is hard on the body. Period."
—Mark Guilliams, strength-and-conditioning coach at NASA

Life in orbit is exhilarating, awe-inspiring, breathtaking . . . and it takes a serious toll on the body. There's a reason why space is often called a "hostile environment," and it's not because of angry aliens. Take a look at some of the things that happen to an astronaut's body in space travel.

YOUR FINGERNAILS CAN FALL OFF. A 2010 study of 232 astronauts found that in 10 percent of cases, tight-fitting, restrictive gloves caused fingernails to break or fall off completely. Because the gloves are built to be extra durable to prevent puncture, they are not flexible. When they are too tight-fitting, they can cut off blood flow to the fingertips.

YOU MIGHT RETURN A LITTLE SQUINTY. "Five years ago," said John Charles, of NASA's Human Research Program, in an interview with NPR, "we had an astronaut on station all of a sudden say, 'Hey, my eyesight has changed. I'm three months into this flight, and I can't read the checklists anymore.'" Astronauts had complained of vision problems upon their return from space for years. The space station was even stocked with adjustable eyeglasses in anticipation of astronauts developing vision changes. Since scientists knew that one of the effects of gravity had been puffy-face syndrome, they wondered if that could also cause pressure to build up on the eyes and even change eye shape. Tests showed that though the pressure increase wasn't very high in space compared to Earth, the problem was that astronauts' brains are never relieved of that pressure in microgravity—the fluid stays up in their heads. "So we now think this mild-but-persistent pressure may be the thing that's stimulating remodeling the eye and causing the visual impairment," said eye doctor Benjamin Levine. Scientists are working with businesses on a solution that's "almost like a sleeping sack or pair of trousers that you can put on at night" that will "hook up to a vacuum cleaner, suck the blood and fluid into the feet, and unload the heart and the brain while you're sleeping," says Levine.

YOU MIGHT NEED TO BREAK OUT THE BARF BAGS. Ever get carsick? Even if you haven't, you might still have a little trouble on a spacecraft. Space sickness is a very real and uncomfortable phenomenon for many astronauts. "Your inner ear thinks you're tumbling; the balance system in there is going all over the place," says retired astronaut Leroy Chiao. "Meanwhile, your eyes are telling you you're not tumbling—you're upright. The two systems are sending all this contradictory information to your brain . . . that's why some people feel nauseous." After a few days, most crew members' bodies adjust to the zero-G environment and the nausea disappears. But for others, like former Senator Jake Garn, it can get pretty bad:

"Jake Garn was pretty sick. I don't know whether we should tell stories like that. But anyway, Jake Garn, he has made a mark in the [NASA] Astronaut Corps because he represents the maximum level of space sickness that anyone can ever attain. And so the mark of being totally sick and totally incompetent is one Garn. Most guys will get maybe to a tenth Garn, *if* that high. And within the Astronaut Corps, he forever will be remembered by that."
— Robert E. Stevenson, NASA astronaut

YOU GROW . . . SORT OF. Scott Kelly grew about two inches taller during a year in space. On Earth, gravity compresses our spines. Without the pull of gravity, the spine lengthens, and voilà! But back on Earth, you'll shrink down again. And you might have some back problems, too, because of lower-back muscles *atrophying*, or weakening, from lack of use. Scientists have recommended adding yoga to space workouts to prevent this.

With muscle and bone loss, the danger of exposure to space radiation that might cause cancer, and more, space travel is serious business. "It was hard, it was exciting, it was scary, it was indescribable," astronaut Marsha Ivins told *Wired* magazine. "And yes, I'd go back in a heartbeat."

"Space is very inhospitable. We explore space for two main reasons: First, humans are so very serious, and our curiosity drives us to explore. When we explore, we are expressing our humanity. Space is kind of the next and last place to explore. Second, just like traveling to a foreign country or even a strange city, when we explore space, our understanding of ourselves, our Earth, and our place in the universe is changed and, I think, improved. I think exploring the cold harsh corners of space helps us understand how lucky we are here on Earth and how valuable and vulnerable our Earth is."

—Adam Steltzner, NASA engineer

FOLDING OUR WAY INTO SPACE

The ancient art of origami may offer solutions to the space-radiation problem. As NASA tries to figure out how to protect astronauts from radiation on extended trips like a voyage to Mars, they are considering the design of a foldable "space blanket" shield. "A lot of people have experience with concepts for folding and unfolding. So even though people don't have a background in space radiation or in material science, many people have backgrounds in design or architecture that may be able to offer us some solutions," says NASA technician Doug Hoffman. Origami has inspired spacecraft design, and NASA's Jet Propulsion Laboratory even had an origami-and-folding spacecraft expert! NASA has also been working on the development of an origami-inspired folding radiator for use on small satellites. Starshade—a NASA project designed using origami principles to facilitate exoplanet photography by blocking bright starlight that hides exoplanets—will fold to a size that can be launched in a rocket and then unfold in space "to a diameter of about 85 feet (26 meters) . . . about the size of a standard baseball diamond." Using origami in this way offers "a lot of magnification in a really tight space," researcher Eric Tremblay told *Popular Science*.

NASA's Jet Propulsion Laboratory sees a bright future for more origami-inspired technology. CubeSats, tiny briefcase-size satellites, may eventually use folding structures that make it easier to pack antennae and equipment. The collapsible PUFFER (pop-up flat-folding explorer robot) was also inspired by origami. It pops open and folds down and has the ability to climb rocks and squeeze into tight spaces. It can accompany rovers and fold into itself to go places that the rovers can't.

"It's Magic Up There"
—Chris Hadfield, commander of International Space Station

The ISS is the largest artificial object in low-Earth orbit, a manmade satellite, engineering marvel, and super science lab.

One day we may want to live on other planets. One day we might not have a choice. "We may eventually need resources from asteroids or the Moon, depending on how we manage the resources we've got here on Earth," writes Charles Fishman in *The Atlantic*. "We may eventually need to become a multi-planet species—either because we literally outgrow the Earth or because we damage it. Or we may simply *want* to become a multiplanet species: One day, some people may prefer the empty black silence of the Moon or the uncrowded red beauty of Mars, just as they preferred Oklahoma to Philadelphia in the 1890s." As we dream of building something

like a new Earth on Mars, it's clear to many that international cooperation is key. Former NASA Administrator Charles Bolden points out that "any mission to Mars is likely to be a global effort."

The ISS is a big part of that global effort. "The International Space Station is this absolutely amazing endeavor," said astronaut Cady Coleman In a conversation with travel expert Rick Steves. "This is 16 different countries, all joined together, flying one vehicle together." In addition to the six people on the spacecraft, "on the ground, there are hundreds of people that are working together every single day, [answering] hard questions together and having to establish relationships." There's a primary partnership between the United States and Russia—each country literally manages its own half of the spacecraft. The US side is controlled by Europe, Canada, and Japan, and it houses a crew member from one of those regions. Most of the operation and navigation responsibilities are shared, and everyone generally works on their side of the station, but they do often get together for meals and breaks. So far, more than 200 people from 18 countries have visited the ISS. "It gives me a lot of faith in people themselves," said Coleman. "We're really all from the same place."

As big as a football field (end zones included), with living quarters comparable to a six-bedroom, two-bathroom house, construction of the ISS began in 1998, and it's expected to be used until 2028. But used how? What exactly is it for? What goes on up there every day? And how the heck do they go to the bathroom in space?

ISS HISTORY

President Reagan and NASA started out with big plans for the ISS. "NASA's original vision for the station was as ambitious as it had been for Apollo or the shuttles," writes Fishman. "The station was to have seven major functions—it was to be a research lab, a manufacturing facility, an observatory, a space transportation hub, a satellite-repair facility, a spacecraft-assembly facility, and a staging base for manned missions to the solar system." As times changed, priorities shifted, and reality replaced dreams. "Thirty years later, just one of those functions remains: research lab. And, Reagan's aspirations notwithstanding, no one today is using materials or medicines invented on the station, let alone manufactured there. Currently, about 40 percent of the station's commercial-research capacity is unused—in part, perhaps, because some companies don't know it's available; in part because others aren't sure how zero-G research would be worthwhile."

"In the course of a year, we do about 400 different scientific experiments on the International Space Station. The zero-G environment is pretty amazing for research."
—Scott Kelly, NASA astronaut

But the research that *is* done is extraordinarily powerful and could possibly offer an enormous amount of hope for the future of human life, as the ISS was built to study the possibilities of life and health in space—

and here on Earth. "I call the International Space Station the world's greatest laboratory," says NASA's Dava Newman.

"engineering in space"

The ISS is about one million pounds of lab, suspended almost 250 miles above Earth, moving at a speed of more than 17,000 miles per hour, and circling the Earth about every 90 minutes, which ends up being around 16 times a day. The ISS zooms "from San Francisco to New York in 9 minutes," says Commander Chris Hadfield. "In 9 minutes, you can see the whole [United States]."

"The Station's made out of about 30 loads that went up by shuttle or Russian rockets," said Piers Sellers. "And somebody had to bolt it all together. And that's what we did, you know—engineering in space." How did it happen? Well, very carefully, for

one. Most of the construction happened between 1998 and 2011, and it was the Space Shuttle program, along with Russia's Soyuz vehicles, that were responsible for carrying it, piece by piece (along with people), up to space. The ISS was built in orbit by a combination of astronauts and robots. The space shuttle Endeavor brought up the ISS's Canadarm and Canadarm2, the main robot arms used to move parts, equipment, and astronauts to build and operate the station. With the retirement of the Space Shuttle program, Russia's small Soyuz vehicles have been the primary mode of transport to the ISS, but commercial spacecraft are getting into the act. "We

reached an agreement with two companies, Boeing and SpaceX, to build two different vehicles that could carry our crews to space. So, they're both building vehicles that can carry up to seven people, like the shuttle used to," says Bolden. "Eventually, NASA will send the crews up through Boeing and SpaceX. They'll dock to the International Space Station and stay for six months or seven months. So we'll do even more research and more science."

"Working in space to construct or repair a spaceship that weighs one million pounds is so challenging that the station's exterior elements have a remarkable engineering feature: Although the station is made up of more than 100 components, with a surface area spanning almost three acres, most bolts the astronauts work with are a single size. That way astronauts almost never have to worry about changing sockets. Imagine constructing a whole building that way. All the scripting, the rehearsal, the design considerations—life in space isn't just stranger than ordinary folks realize; it's harder. Harder even than NASA has always imagined."

—"5,200 Days in Space,"
Charles Fishman, *The Atlantic*

By operating in low-Earth orbit, which is safer than outer space, researchers can conduct in-depth, long-term studies of the kinds of spacecraft, conditions, and tools humans will need for long missions to places like Mars. Even though it's complicated, it's still our best shot.

FUN FACT The ISS is so big that you don't need a telescope to see it in the night sky. And there are a number of apps, like ISS Spotter, that will help anyone find and track it. Want to track the ISS? Visit n2yo.com!

THE DAILY GRIND

Working on the ISS is not exactly a 9-to-5 job. Countries are allocated specific amounts of research time depending on how much money or resources they've contributed to the ISS. The crew is very, very busy. Even in space, they can't get out of a good ol' group meeting: "Every day starts and ends with a daily planning conference, during which the astronauts briefly check in with all five control centers around the world to talk about schedule glitches or pending maintenance, or to look ahead to the next day." All of their activities are carefully planned and monitored by Mission Control, and most of their time is spent maintaining the spacecraft itself and conducting research. NASA believes that the capacity for long-term human health research on the ISS is critical for future missions across the solar system, like NASA's planned Journey to Mars.

Scott Kelly points out that "in space, your body recognizes that it doesn't need a skeleton to support your weight anymore, so, hey, let's just get rid of it. So in 100 months . . . theoretically, you would have no bones left." Research has already shown that space is a hostile environment, and microgravity affects human eyes, muscles, bones, and cardiovascular systems in significant ways.

Astronauts also test out commercial products, like 3-D printers, and work on growing edibles in space. In 2015, the Expedition 44 crew harvested the first space crop: "outredgeous" red romaine lettuce grown in the ISS greenhouse. The seeds had been "planted" by Expedition 39 in 2014. "There is evidence that supports that fresh foods, such as tomatoes, blueberries, and red lettuce, are a good source of antioxidants. Having fresh food like these available in space could have a positive impact on people's moods and also could provide some protection against radiation in space," says NASA's Ray Wheeler. NASA also believes that the ability to grow food in space could have psychological benefits. "Having something green and growing—a little piece of Earth—to take care of when living and working in an extreme and stressful environment could have tremendous value and impact."

In the microgravity environment on the ISS, there's all kinds of research going on—Earth and space science, astronomy, physics, biotechnology, materials science, biomedical technology—the list goes on and on. "Most of the experiments that we do are physics, biology, chemistry. For example, fluid physics, or understanding more efficient combustion," says astronaut Scott Kelly. "Crystals are able to be grown in space that are perfect," points out Bolden. "So if you're looking at producing pharmaceuticals, we can better look at the structure of a drug."

Medical research is an important part of the work on the ISS. As scientists study what happens to astronauts' bodies in space, they will develop an understanding of the possibilities and consequences of long spaceflights—like the six to eight months it would take to get to Mars. Since there is not usually a medical doctor on the ISS, remote ultrasound technology allows for the study and treatment of medical conditions there. Such research might also help develop systems for medical care in areas where access to doctors is a challenge, such as remote or rural areas.

Osteoporosis, an illness that weakens bones, is the subject of much research on the ISS. "When we go up there, we lose bone . . . at about 10 times the rate of a woman who has osteoporosis who's about 70 years old. What she loses in a whole year, I lose in a month if I'm not doing something to stop it." On the ISS, astronauts are part of experiments studying the condition. They are also subjects of a study of heart function, because hearts get "lazy" in microgravity.

On the ISS, spacecraft systems are also tested in preparation for longer, more complicated space voyages. Crews are not only responsible for science but also for maintaining the station. Sometimes this requires that they venture on spacewalks to perform repairs.

Astronaut Coleman points out that other vital research is *only* possible in space. "Things like *combustion*

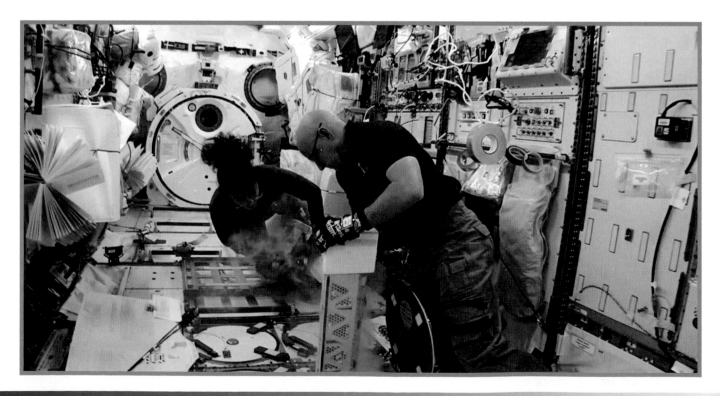

Experiment being conducted on the International Space Station

[or burning] . . . things burn a little differently up there . . . more slowly. It allows us to study the process . . . we're learning about pollution, soot production."

In addition, astronauts communicate and exchange information with teams and schools on Earth, like when ISS astronaut Scott Tingle spent time chatting with students and alumni of his alma mater, the University of Massachusetts at Dartmouth. Though life on the ISS has its challenges, Tingle seems to be loving it. He told students, "The days are full, and they're busy, and [they're] some of the most rewarding days I've ever had." Tingle added that "we're living as humans in space, and that's always a challenge because it's not our natural environment. We make it as natural as we can." For those who want to follow in his footsteps or embark on a path of their own, Tingle says, "Set a course, set a goal, and don't be afraid of where the journey brings you. You will have some barriers that you will have to go over or go around, or you may change your mind, but if you've got a plan, you can work it and you will get there."

The ISS crew provides other opportunities for students on Earth by conducting experiments that students have developed, providing lessons for classroom use, and, like Tingle, connecting directly to them via e-mail, radio, or videoconferencing. The Amateur Radio on the ISS (ARISS) program lets students talk directly to crew with the hopes of "inspiring them to pursue interests in careers in science, technology, engineering, and math." The European Space Agency offers "Spaceflight Challenge I"—an interactive set of exercises in which students can take on the roles of ISS crew members.

WALKING ON AIR

One of the most useful things on the ISS: Velcro! A 1940s Swiss invention, it's become associated with the space program since the Apollo missions because of its unique way of "holding it down." For now, Velcro is doing its job, but NASA is working on new "sticky" technology inspired by geckos. Geckos have little, hairlike grippers on their feet that help them stick to things, and the stickiness *never* wears off or leaves any residue. NASA created a sticking material with tiny gecko-like hairs on it. When force is applied, the hairs make it stick. Astronauts could use these artificial gecko grippers to hang photos, clipboards, and more. In the future, robots on the ISS could be equipped with these grippers for exterior ISS repair work.

"Once you've been weightless for half a year, you resent gravity a little more."
—Chris Hadfield, commander of International Space Station

The gravity on the ISS is about 90 percent of what it is on the surface of the Earth. "In other words, if a person who weighed 100 pounds on Earth's surface could climb a ladder all the way to the space station, that person would weigh 90 pounds at the top of the ladder," reports NASA. Even though it's only a slight difference, that small change means the difference between standing on your bed playing air guitar and doing it literally.

Zero-G? Is there really NO gravity in space? There's actually a small amount of gravity everywhere in space. We often use the terms *zero-G*, *microgravity*, and *weightlessness* to mean the same thing—that astronauts float because they're in a constant state of free fall. Because of gravity, all objects, no matter their size or weight, will fall at the same rate in a vacuum. "If a person drops a hammer and a feather, air will make the feather fall more slowly. But if there were no air, they would fall at the same acceleration . . . The spacecraft, its crew, and any objects aboard are all falling not toward but *around* Earth. Since they are all falling together, the crew and objects appear to float when compared with the spacecraft."

Astronaut Sandra Magnus got a real lower-body workout (and calluses on her big toes) when she had to move around in microgravity. "I learned to carry things with my knees—tuck them between my knees and shove off. That way I had my hands free to propel myself," she says. "The thing is, in space, Newton's laws rule your life. If you're doing something as simple as typing on a laptop, you're exerting force on the keyboard, and you end up getting pushed away and floating off. You have to hold yourself down with your feet."

Things float away and get lost, so a lot of time has to be spent in keeping them secure—duct tape

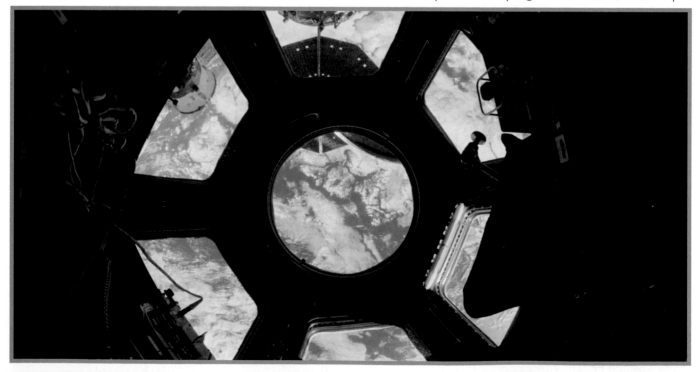

A look at Earth from inside the International Space Station

comes in handy on the ISS. Even so, astronaut Piers Sellers lost a spatula (used for research, not pancakes) on one of his EVAs. "No sign of the spatula, guys, it is gone, gone, gone," he said. "That was my favorite spatch . . . don't tell the other spatulas."

Speaking of pancakes, preparing food on the ISS presents particular challenges, even for simple things like waste disposal. "Gravity lets you throw things in the trash," says Magnus. "Without gravity, you have to figure out what to do. I put the trash on a piece of duct tape—duct tape is awesome—but even dealing with the trash takes forever."

PUTTING IT IN, GETTING IT OUT

"You can't sit, and there's no down." —Chris Hadfield, commander of International Space Station

"Nobody I know goes for the food." —Cady Coleman, NASA astronaut

"Space food in popular culture ranges from liquid meals of various viscosities—think Stanley Kubrick's *2001: A Space Odyssey*," reports CNN, "to a miracle pill containing a day's worth of nutrition." The reality, at times, has been close. John Glenn showed the world that it was possible to digest food in space. Unfortunately, on the 1962 Friendship 7 mission, all he had for his first "meal" was applesauce and water with sugar tablets—not exactly a feast. He went on to "enjoy" a tube of beef and vegetables, a meal that he squeezed right into his mouth, like toothpaste. In the early days of space travel, the army-style pureed food was far from gourmet. Project Gemini brought with it freeze-dried and dehydrated food that was coated in gelatin and oils for preservation. This way of preparing food meant it could be kept for long periods at room temperature. The freeze-dried food got rehydrated in its packet with cold water from a water gun, and then . . . bon appétit! Um, yay?

In December 1964, the *Los Angeles Times* reported that "eating conventionally from a plate with a knife and fork is out of the question in space . . . An astronaut drinking coffee from a cup would never get the liquid to his lips; the coffee would dance in the air in front of him as he tipped the cup. When Scott Carpenter tried to eat cookies on his flight, the crumbs stayed behind to float in front of his face like so many large particles of dust."

Perhaps in rebellion against what manager of NASA's Space Food Systems Lab, Vickie Kloeris, calls "cubes and tubes," astronaut John Young caused what might have been the first "space scandal" on the Gemini 3 mission. He snuck a corned-beef-on-rye sandwich aboard, tucked into his pocket just before launch. In flight, he offered to share it with crew member Gus Grissom. According to Space.com, the mission transcript records a brief conversation about this ultimately unsuccessful caper:

"What is it?" Grissom asked.

"Corned-beef sandwich," Young replied.

"Where did that come from?" Grissom asked.

Answered Young: "I brought it with me. Let's see how it tastes. Smells, doesn't it?"

Grissom tasted the sandwich but quickly announced that he would stick it back in his pocket, because it was starting to break up. Young suggested the sandwich was "a thought . . . not a very good one."

Replied Grissom: "Pretty good, though, if it would just hold together."

Maybe Young was desperate—he knew that the astronauts' meals were highly regulated. *Smithsonian* reports that the Gemini astronauts were allowed to have 2,500 calories a day during space missions—down from their normal 3,000—because they were less active in space. "The food, which had 99 percent of the moisture removed to reduce weight, had an average content of 17 percent protein, 32 percent fat, and 51 percent carbohydrates."

The Apollo missions added hot water and 300 calories, upping the calorie allotment to 2,800. The food was freeze-dried in a process described by the Smithsonian National Air and Space Museum:

"Prior to packaging, a food was quick-frozen and then placed into a vacuum chamber. The vacuum removed all moisture from the foods. They were then packaged while still in the vacuum chamber. Freeze-drying provides foods that will keep their nutrition and taste qualities almost indefinitely. They are extremely light and compact and require no refrigeration."

Rehydrated food was contained in a "spoon bowl,"

says Kloeris, so astronauts "could use a utensil for the first time." After ingesting things like rehydrated pineapple fruit cake, crew members had to place special tablets in the food bags in order to prevent the growth of bacteria. For the most part, things had improved since the Gemini days, though some Apollo astronauts complained that they were given too much food and that it was "too sweet." By Apollo 11, astronauts had a mixture of preplanned meals plus access to a pantry where they could choose from a variety of foods and drink, including orange drink, bacon squares, shrimp cocktail (a favorite), spaghetti with meat sauce, and scalloped potatoes. Apollo 15 astronauts enjoyed steak and eggs for breakfast. Bacon squares were a perennial favorite; strawberry cubes were not.

FUN FACT Every year, NASA offers students an opportunity for a "Top Chef" in space type of competition. The Astronaut Culinary Challenge announces an annual theme, and schools can develop corresponding recipes that will pass muster at the NASA Johnson Space Center Food Lab. The winning entries are prepared and processed, then sent up to real astronauts on the ISS! So far, the ISS crew has enjoyed things like Jamaican rice and peas and strawberry rhubarb crisp. Want to try? Check out the Astronaut Culinary Challenge here: https://nasahunch.com/culinary-challenge/

FUN FACT Though John Glenn made Tang the "astronaut's drink" when he drank it as part of the research on Friendship 7 in 1962, it had actually been developed in 1957 for anyone to enjoy—not just the space program.

By 1973, on Skylab, things were looking up—or at least, things could be held down. Astronauts used forks and spoons and even had a designated dining area. In the past, if astronauts were eating peas, "you have to move the spoon to your mouth in one smooth motion. If you stop your hand for some reason, the peas keep right on traveling—individually." But on Skylab, the peas were in a special sauce that held them together. Skylab had a galley where the astro-

nauts could prepare and cook their food. It was equipped with a refrigerator and used solar cells for power instead of fuel. Most food on Skylab was frozen or canned. "Instead of being rehydrated, food items packaged in pop-top aluminum cans or plastic pouches were heated in these containers before consumption," reports the Smithsonian National Air and Space Museum. One big hit came because of the refrigeration: ice cream! Astronauts enjoyed their snacks, and a 1972 article in the *Saturday Review* reported that "one four-man crew in a space simulation ate 800 chocolate bars in 90 days." For most meals, though, astronauts could enjoy a frozen dinner on a dining tray, which doubled as an oven to heat the food. Kloeris points out that Skylab "was the most sophisticated food system that NASA's ever flown," as it was the first and only time NASA had food-only freezers in orbit.

The Apollo-Soyuz Test Project allowed US astronauts a taste of the finest in tubed borscht and caviar.

During the space shuttle days of the '80s, much of the astronauts' fare was just what you'd find in a local grocery store but often repackaged or freeze-dried to be *shelf stable*, or able to last a long time at room temperatures. Astronauts Velcro'ed meal trays to their thighs to act as tabletops (and food packets were Velcro'ed to the trays) and used magnetic utensils. In the '90s, as missions got longer, new packaging and disposal systems were developed, including a trash compactor.

"The food system for [the ISS] will be considerably different from the shuttle food system. Since the electrical power for [the ISS] will be from solar panels, there is no extra water generated onboard. Water will be recycled from the cabin air, but that will not be enough for use in the food system. Most of the food planned for [the ISS] will be frozen, refrigerated, or thermostabilized and will not require the addition of water before consumption. Many of the beverages will be in the dehydrated form. Food will be heated to serving temperature in a microwave/forced-air convection oven. One oven will be supplied for each group of four astronauts."
—from a **NASA ISS spaceflight fact sheet**

On the ISS, there's no food refrigeration, so food still has to be specially packaged as well as dehydrated on Earth and rehydrated in space. All food (and packaging) that goes on the ISS has to be tested. There are thermostabilized foods, which are similar to canned foods but are packaged differently in a process that combines heat and pressure to make the food "commercially sterile." "It's called a flexible can or a *retort pouch*," says Kloeris. "It's really the canning process . . . that your grandmother or great-grandmother did." Some food is eaten in its natural form, like fruit and cereals like Fruity Pebbles. There's an oven, though food can only be heated to room temperature, and there are even condiments like mustard and ketchup. "Alongside such healthy dishes as Indian fish curry and crab cakes, the NASA menu includes chocolate pudding, lemon-curd cake, and apricot cobbler. NASA has even been known to send birthday cakes for astronauts." Though there are treats, nutritionists carefully plan the astronauts' diets, making sure they get a balanced supply of calories, vitamins, and minerals. And about reduce,

reuse, recycle? NASA reports that "as on Earth, space food comes in disposable packages. Astronauts must throw their packages away when they have finished eating. Some packaging actually prevents food from flying away. The food packaging is designed to be flexible and easier to use, as well as to maximize space when stowing or disposing of food containers."

Astronauts on the ISS get three kinds of food. First, there's *daily-menu food*—the regular breakfast, lunch, and dinner stuff. "The packaging system for the daily-menu food is based on single-service, disposable containers. Food items will be packaged as individual servings to facilitate inflight changes and substitutions to preselected menus. Single-service containers also eliminate the need for a dishwasher." Next there's *safe-haven food*, which is for emergencies. It's enough to sustain a crew for 22 days, has a long shelf life, and is designed to take up minimal volume and weight. And finally, there's *EVA food* for those eight-hour spacewalks. For EVAs, each crew member gets 38 ounces of water and 500 calories of food in refillable containers. To avoid the crumb situation that John Young had with the corned beef on rye, Hadfield says that soft tortilla wraps are often used in place of bread.

"Unless they're participating in a medical experiment," says Kloeris, crew members are "not going to be tracking exactly what they eat every day." But NASA's nutrition-research lab does provide them with a computerized "food-frequency question-naire." Kloeris adds that crew members input "estimates of how many servings from each category they have consumed during that week" to track calories, salt, water intake, and more. Because a typical scale wouldn't work in a microgravity environment, the ISS crew sits in a mass-measuring device to keep track of weight fluctuations. The medical team can use this data to help the crew stay healthy.

FUN FACT The Russian side of the ISS uses canned foods, which are eaten on tables with built-in warming devices. Kloeris says that since both the US and Russian sides share food, the Russians use a type of portable warming briefcase to warm the NASA food pouches.

FUN FACT Though there are no refrigerators for food on the ISS, there is one for biological samples used in science research and experiments. Not the place for grabbing a midnight snack!

FUN FACT Salt and pepper are used on the ISS in liquid form—salt crystals and pepper flakes would not be pleasant for crew members' eyes!

a common scent

Astronauts on the ISS take daily sponge baths (using a squirt gun), and they have a special rinse-free shampoo for their hair. Apparently there's no problem with body odor. They don't get too dirty, anyway—the ISS is a very clean environment and "clothes never really touch you up there . . . clothes just float near you," says Hadfield. "They don't pick up the oils and odor from your body."

Yes, astronauts do drink their own pee. "The ISS is a closed life-support system," says astronaut Peggy Whitson. "So we're collecting our energy with solar panels. That provides the energy, for instance, to take our water and break it into oxygen and hydrogen. We, also, are losing a lot of water through our bodies, through condensation, from our breath, and through sweating and urinating. We collect all that, process it, and make it clean again, make it drinkable. And then the excess of that we use to break apart and make more oxygen."

Going to the bathroom "takes practice," says

Hadfield . . . and something like a special vacuum cleaner. "In place of gravity we have air flow, which pulls everything down into the toilet. You pee into one tube that has a big yellow funnel on the end. It has air pulled into it, and that runs through a big sewage system with centrifuges and filters and purifiers, and then at the other end of that is the tap that you drink out of." Solid waste "goes into a thing that looks like a big milk can." Each can gets sealed in a cloth bag that prevents odors from escaping. When enough cans are accumulated, the poop is ejected into space, where it burns up (and hopefully doesn't stink up the universe).

Family, Fun, and Games

Though it's a challenging life for the crew on the ISS, there are telephones and special iPads for communicating with family and friends, as well as psychologists and strength coaches who help the astronauts maintain their mental and physical health.

 Coleman says that packing for a mission happens about a year in advance, and the bag is very light. "About six pairs of pants and 12 shirts for six months . . . [and] gym clothes for working out."

Astronauts sleep while floating in special sleeping bags that are attached to the wall. Instead of bedhead, Coleman says astronauts get "space hair."

The astronauts have a couple of hours each day for exercise and recreation. Even though the space station is fully supplied with books and movies, astronaut Ed Lu decided to spend his limited free time doing other things, like acrobatics in microgravity. "I don't know if I'm ever coming back here," Lu said in an interview. "I want to do things I can never do at home."

Astronauts have small cubicles/cabins with doors for privacy, where they can have private conversations with family and sleep. The ISS agreed to operate on Universal (UTC)/Greenwich Mean Time (GMT) to best accommodate the international crew in space and on the ground.

"This is the hardest thing we've ever done," says Kelly, "and if we can do this, we can do anything. We just have to dream it, and dream big, and go do it. And that's . . . [the] perspective you get when you're able to spend time in space and look out at the planet we have."

Just getting to Mars will take about six to eight months, so NASA is working to make sure that we can thrive when we get there. "Before we launch our mission to Mars, we're trying to make sure that we know that all of our life-support systems are functioning right," says Bolden.

"The International Space Station showed that humanity can, in fact, work together," says Bolden. "That in spite of everything else that's going on down here on this planet, when you really focus on a particular mission, you work pretty well together."

FUN FACT While she was on the ISS, astronaut Cady Coleman performed a flute duet with Ian Anderson of rock band Jethro Tull.

SETTING RECORDS . . . IN SPACE

Jim Voss and Susan Helms have participated in the longest EVA so far, spacewalking for 8 hours and 56 minutes doing ISS construction work in 2001.

Mike Fincke holds the US record for most time in space: 381 ½ days over a span of three missions. He has done 48 hours of spacewalking. He is also the first to become a dad in space—when his wife went into labor during a 2004 mission, Mission Control connected him to her cellphone!

Scott Kelly holds the US record for longest consecutive time in space (340 days) which he completed in 2015 and 2016. While he was there, he also took part in a "twin study" along with his Earth-bound twin brother, Mark, whose feet remained firmly on solid ground.

Peggy Whitson holds the records for most time spent in space (665 days) and the longest spaceflight (289 days on the ISS) by a woman.

House party! The biggest number of people in space at once is 13, which happened for the first time on the Endeavor mission in 2009.

ISS IN CYBERSPACE

"Launch was awesome!!" astronaut Mike Massimino tweeted in 2009. In the first tweet from space, @Astro_Mike also wrote, "I am feeling great, working hard, & enjoying the magnificent views, the adventure of a lifetime has begun!"

In May 2013, ISS commander Chris Hadfield shot a music video of David Bowie's song "Space Oddity" from the ISS. The first music video ever filmed in space "in a little one-guy recording studio" is now available on YouTube!

In November 2017, ESA's Paolo Nespoli took a side gig as a Wikipedia contributor while he worked on the ISS, making two recordings (in English and Italian) of his voice. This was the first Wiki content made from space.

JAMES WEBB SPACE TELESCOPE

A collaboration between NASA, the European Space Agency, and the Canadian Space Agency is being designed to work in part as the Hubble Telescope's successor. With the high-resolution James Webb Space Telescope, not only will we be able to see farther out, but we'll see more detail and get more information. Development began in 1996, and it was eventually named after James E. Webb, NASA's second administrator. "We're going to launch the James Webb Space Telescope," says Stofan. "James Webb is actually going to be able to start looking at the atmospheres of these planets. It's going to look for things like water vapor, carbon dioxide, [and] methane—gases that here on this planet are consistent with the presence of life." The James Webb Space Telescope has been jokingly called a time machine because it will allow us to see celestial objects at great distances and allow us to observe the births of galaxies, planets, and stars. "It's almost like looking at the beginning of that evolutionary process and the details of how we got here," says Lee Feinberg, an optical telescope element manager at NASA. The James Webb Space Telescope, scheduled to launch in 2020, may tell us more than we ever imagined about how the universe began.

JOURNEY TO MARS

"Kids today . . . are the Mars generation. Someone from their age group will be the first person to walk on Mars—and possibly discover evidence of past life there!"

—Ellen Stofan, former chief scientist at NASA

Ever since we discovered that there really were no little green men, NASA has been working on getting humans to Mars. In 2010, the NASA Authorization Act set goals of sending humans to an asteroid by 2025 and to Mars sometime in the 2030s. After all, it looks like Mars may have supported life in the past.

So what are our prospects for living on Mars in the future? Robots like the Opportunity and Curiosity rovers are working to figure that out right now. NASA scientists and engineers, along with their global partners, are doing work on the ground to plan future robotic and human exploration of the red planet.

The Mars Rover dropping from the Curiosity Rover with a jetpack strapped to it

"I think NASA's big next push will be getting humans to Mars. This will be hard to do; it takes six to eight months to get to Mars, and landing on the surface is a challenge because of Mars's thin atmosphere. But just like with the Apollo Program that got humans to the Moon, we know that when you push technology for space, you get all sorts of benefits to Earth—including lots of the technology that now shows up in our cellphones! So we will go to Mars to see if life ever evolved on the red planet, but this big push will give us huge benefits right here on Earth." —Ellen Stofan, former chief scientist at NASA

"NASA is building a rocket called the Space Launch System, which is going to be bigger than the Saturn V, the rocket that launched astronauts to the Moon," says Ellen Stofan. "We'll launch humans with it for the first time in the early 2020s. And then we're going to build what we call a deep-space habitat, and that's the transfer vehicle that humans will live in on that journey to Mars."

Alyssa Carson has been ready for her journey to Mars for a long time. At three, she told her father, "Daddy, I want to be an astronaut and be one of the people that go to Mars." By 16 years old, the Louisiana native had seen three space shuttle launches. She also attended "Space Camp seven times, Space Academy three times, Robotics Academy once," and multiple Sally Ride Science Junior Academies. Alyssa was also the youngest to graduate from Advanced Space Academy. In 2012 and 2013, she furthered her education at Space Camp Turkey and Space Camp Canada—this made Alyssa the first person to attend all three international NASA Space Camp locations. She's also the first and only person to visit all 14 of NASA's Visitor's Centers across nine states. Alyssa became the youngest to graduate from Advanced PoSSUM Space Academy in 2016—that means she's an official astronaut trainee and certified to go to space!

ASKING AND ANSWERING: MARS CURIOSITY ROVER

Launched in November 2011, Curiosity is an unmanned spacecraft sent to Mars to answer a big question: Did Mars ever support *microbial life* (minute life-form)? By studying the rocks and soil on Mars and investigating the planet's climate and geology, Curiosity can learn a lot about the planet's past and help us figure out what is possible in the future. Curiosity's mission is unprecedented in many ways.

First of all, the machine is HUGE (for a rover). It's about twice as long and five times as heavy as NASA's Spirit and Opportunity Mars rovers, which were launched in 2003.

Second, it made a big entrance. NASA engineer Adam Steltzner remembers, "We hit the atmosphere fast enough to burn up, so we wrapped the Curiosity rover in a shell that will smolder and not burn. The process of hitting the atmosphere slows us down to about 1,000 miles an hour . . . Then, we open up the world's largest supersonic parachute—a parachute the size of a house. That slows us down to a couple hundred miles an hour but not slow enough to land. So then the rover—with a jet backpack on top of it— drops away from the parachute and lights these rockets up." A tether lowered Curiosity to the

Close-up shot of the Mars Rover still in the Curiosity Rover

surface, allowing it to land on its wheels. And then NASA "cut the jet backpack free."

Curiosity landed on August 6, 2012, and has kept on chugging ever since, already lasting three times longer than intended.

FUN FACT Though there have been rumors that Curiosity sings "Happy Birthday" to itself every year, the rover set things straight on social media. In a 2017 tweet, the rover said, "The reports of my singing are greatly exaggerated. I only hummed 'Happy Birthday' to myself once, back in 2013." Scientists programmed the rover to vibrate at different frequencies; the vibrations in a particular sequence could be considered "singing."

FAST FACT Amazing as Curiosity is, *Gizmodo* reported that the iPhone 4S was four times more powerful than the rover!

Once it got there, Curiosity was able to do more than any of the rovers before it. Curiosity can "roll over obstacles up to 25 inches (65 cm) high and travel about 660 feet (200 m) per day." With drills, high-resolution cameras, and other equipment to analyze samples from Mars's surface, Curiosity has already sent us an incredible amount of information

and thousands of images (including a selfie!). "The complexity of the Curiosity rover, in terms of being able to get samples and analyze them, is really amazing," says Michael Watkins, Director of NASA's Jet Propulsion Laboratory. "What we basically gave it was an analytical chemistry lab. It's really the first time we've had anything like that on any planet. It

drills into the rock, makes powder, and then is able to drop off into some inlets, where instruments can then do more complicated analysis."

And what Curiosity did very quickly was tell us that, at some point, there was probably water—drinkable, liquid water—on Mars.

"What Curiosity was able to find—even fairly early in the mission—was types of rocks that only form in water over long periods of time. It was able to find minerals that indicate that that water was persistent and that that water was the kind of water you could reach down and take a drink out of. And that is one of the holy grails of habitability."
—Michael Watkins, director of NASA Jet Propulsion Laboratory

"Curiosity has answered our question," continues Watkins. "And that answer is yes—the ancient wet environment, three-and-a-half billion years ago, when life was first starting here on Earth . . . Mars was an environment that was habitable for life. So that's pretty darn cool."

FAST FACT All abuzz! While the rovers on Mars have gathered an incredible amount of valuable information, they are a little . . . slow. So NASA is working on a solution: robot bees! Researchers in the US and Japan are working on developing these tiny robots, called Marsbees. "Marsbees are robotic flapping wing flyers of a bumblebee size with cicada-sized wings," reports NASA. "The larger wings are needed because of Mars's thin atmosphere." Engadget reports that "they would travel in swarms, enabling these robotic creatures to fly into Mars's atmosphere, survey the planet, and take a wide range of readings, thanks to their mobility."

WHAT DO ROCKS TELL US?

Space geologist Adriana Ocampo would probably answer "A LOT." Ocampo studies rocks on planets and other planetary objects like moons to learn more about their history and formation. Rocks are basically a record of a planet's history, telling the story of a world's past. The deeper they are in the ground, then, generally, the older they are. Ocampo has studied *crater formation*—holes that are caused when something crashes into a planet—on Mars. Ocampo can find out what happened to cause the craters just by studying them! But her research isn't limited to outer space. For instance, Ocampo helped discover a crater on Earth (in Chicxulub, Mexico) that was caused by an asteroid or comet crash about 65 million years ago. In fact, this "Crater of Doom" may have been what caused the massive climate disruption that zapped out all the dinosaurs!

Ocampo's dream of working for NASA began in childhood, in her home of Buenos Aires, Argentina. She wrote a letter to NASA to inquire about a job. When her family moved to California, she got involved with a NASA Space Explorers project through her high school. She eventually went on to work for the Jet Propulsion Laboratory after she graduated high school. When she was only 21 years old, she programmed the cameras that traveled on the Viking spacecraft and was one of the very first people to see the Viking images sent back from Mars.

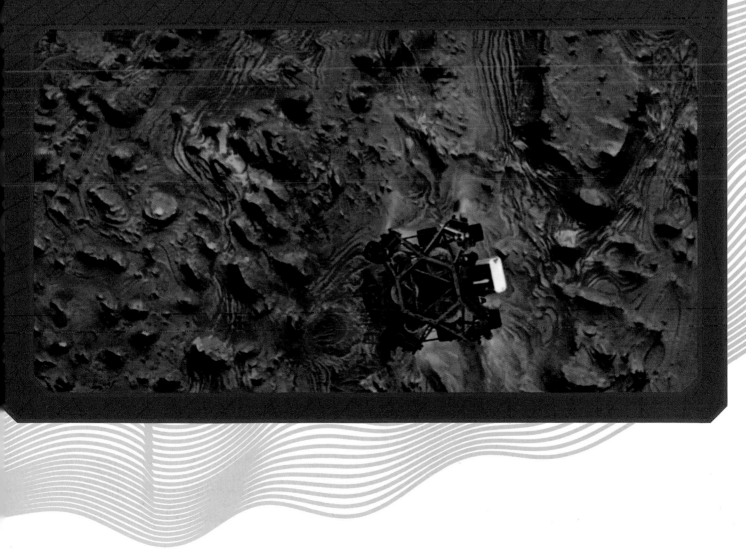

SUN
SOLAR DYNAMICS OBSERVATORY

WHAT'S ON THE MARS MENU?

Not an easy question to answer, considering that "the red planet's frigid average temperature is around −80°F and its thin atmosphere is comprised of 95.32 percent carbon dioxide," reports *Inhabitat*. Maya Cooper—a senior researcher at the Space Food Systems Laboratory in Johnson Space Center—is working to answer that question. And we've come a long way from squeeze-tube food. "We need new approaches," said Cooper in an interview with NBC.

Space Safety magazine reports that "a trip to the Martian surface offers some flexibility over orbital missions, since Mars's gravity could allow visitors to chop vegetables and boil water." The magazine continues, "The simplest approach to feeding astronauts on a Mars mission would be the same way ISS crews are fed now: Load up their ship with prepackaged meals . . . foods would need to be developed with shelf lives years longer than the current two-year standard to avoid spoilage during the trip." And they'd have to carry a LOT of food. "For flights on space shuttles and the International Space Station, astronauts get 3.8 pounds of food per day. For a five-year, round-trip mission to Mars, that would mean almost 7,000 pounds of food per person," reports NBC. Cooper and her Advanced Food Technology team are developing recipes that could be prepared by astronauts on Mars, so they wouldn't have to rely on prepackaged meals. They hope to help develop a system where astronauts will grow their own food, particularly plants that are low-maintenance and don't take up too much space. Think lettuce, strawberries, carrots, spinach . . . the healthy stuff!

As NASA plans for the 2020 launch of the James Webb Space Telescope and new information from the Curiosity rover that might lead to the possibility of Mars-bound vacations for all, Newman is hopeful for the agency's future. "I see a great future for NASA and aerospace in general. There will be many people in space . . . followed by getting astronauts and many rovers back to the Moon, and then we will successfully send humans to Mars and return them to Earth safely. In the next decade, we might find the evidence of life (past or present) somewhere else in the universe. And we will definitely discover thousands more exoplanets. We will gain insight into dark energy and dark matter, which accounts for most of the universe. NASA will work in partnership with aerospace companies and universities to accomplish these exciting space discoveries and exploration. [NASA's aeronautics program] is also superexciting, and we're working on research for supersonic and hypersonic flight. Finally, NASA's contribution to studying . . . Earth is absolutely critical and essential in the next decade so that we can start regenerating Earth's subsystems: oceans, land, and air."

As we continue to look for ways to preserve and protect our lives on this planet, Newman believes that NASA has an important role to play. "A few of NASA's biggest challenges in the future are to remain innovative, to invest in early-stage research and technology, to lead the world's space agencies, and to endeavor for global peaceful exploration rather than to lose its leadership role." Steltzner adds that "when we here at NASA explore, we're really doing it for humanity. It's a celebration of our human curiosity and it's a celebration of what we humans are capable of."

"When I think of NASA, to me, it embodies all the best things about the human race: our desire to know what's beyond the next hill, our desire to understand the world we live in, and our desire to take that information and to use it to help humankind."

—Ellen Stofan, former chief scientist at NASA

When President Kennedy asked Congress and the country to take a giant leap of faith and support the US space program in its quest to go above and beyond anything the country had ever done before, he knew that it would require a continued thirst for knowledge, courage, and imagination. "That challenge is one that we're willing to accept, one we are unwilling to postpone, and one we intend to win," he said in 1962. Over the past 60 years, NASA has been at the forefront of taking giant leaps for humankind, in the name of science, in the name of curiosity, and in the name of our future. "For centuries, humankind has looked to the sky to set the stage for a future that redefines our limits and a reality where anything is possible," wrote President Obama.

"Curiosity is such a powerful force. Without it, we wouldn't be who we are today. Curiosity is the passion that drives us through our everyday lives. We have become explorers and scientists with our need to ask questions and to wonder."
—Clara Ma, 12-year-old winner of the Mars Science Laboratory Naming Contest

Sixty years ago, we challenged ourselves to put a man on the Moon. Today, NASA reminds us that space exploration helps us face challenges of protecting our lives here on Earth. "The Earth is a complex planet with interconnected systems," says Stofan. "It is critical to monitor our planet from space, where we can obtain a unique perspective on our at- mosphere, oceans, and land surfaces. It is also critical to continue more detailed measurements on the sur- face of Earth, but combining these measurements with space-based data gives us powerful information to understand our changing planet."

What's next for NASA? Why do scientists spend so much time on these projects, technologies, and

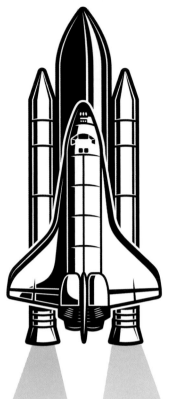

research? Why should we care? We ask questions like these for the same reasons that we want to know about our ancestors, and even our reason for existence. Perhaps the more we discover about our Earth and beyond, the more we'll learn about ourselves, and how to live even more productive lives. "I still have the same sense of wonder about our space program that I did as a child," wrote President Obama in 2016. "It represents an essential part of our character—curiosity and exploration, innovation and ingenuity, pushing the boundaries of what's possible and doing it before anybody else. The space race we won not only contributed immeasurably important technological and medical advances, but it also inspired a new generation of scientists and engineers with the right stuff to keep America on the cutting edge."

Will we build new communities on Mars? Will we come together to protect life on Earth? Where did we start? Where will we end? While our questions may be infinite, it's clear that NASA plans to continue to go above and beyond, to pursue answers to these questions, "not because they are easy, but because they are hard," as President Kennedy said. Because the opportunities to learn and grow are as deep and wide as our universe itself, NASA plans to continue making and meeting new challenges, and going wherever our curiosity takes us.

EAGLE NEBULA
7000 LIGHT-YEARS

BIBLIOGRAPHY

BOOKS

Rise of the Rocket Girls: The Women Who Propelled Us, From Missiles to the Moon, to Mars; Nathalie Holt
We Could Not Fail: The First African Americans in the Space Program; Richard Paul and Steven Moss

NASA STRUCTURE

NASA Centers and Facilities
https://www.nasa.gov/about/sites/index.html
How NASA Works
Craig Freudenrich, PhD
https://science.howstuffworks.com/nasa.htm
WHAT IS NASA?
https://www.nasa.gov/audience/forstudents/k-4/stories/
nasa-knows/what-is-nasa-k4.html
https://www.nasa.gov/audience/forstudents/5-8/features/
nasa-knows/what-is-nasa-58.html

NASA PEOPLE

https://twitter.com/NASApeople
"STEM Role Model Spotlight" Mamta Patel Nagaraja,
National Girls Collaborative Project
Mamta Patel Nagaraja
https://solarsystem.nasa.gov/people/3151/mamta-patel-nagaraja
https://ngcproject.org/blog/stem-role-model-spotlight
-mamta-patel-nagaraja

ENGINEERING

"What's An Engineer? + The Engineering Process: Crash
Course Kids"
Sabrina Cruz explains
http://thekidshouldseethis.com/post/whats-an-engineer-the
-engineering-process-crash-course-kids
"What Is An Engineer?"
http://tryengineering.org/ask-expert/what-engineer
"What Is Engineering?"
Jim Lucas, Live Science, August 21, 2014
https://www.livescience.com/47499-what-is-engineering.html

NASA HISTORY

"The Wright Brothers: Inventing a Flying Machine"
https://airandspace.si.edu/exhibitions/wright-brothers/online/
fly/1903/triumph.cfm
A Brief History of Rocketry, NASA Spacelink System
https://science.ksc.nasa.gov/history/rocket-history.txt
"Why can't an airplane just fly into space? Why do we need
rockets?"
https://spaceplace.nasa.gov/review/dr-marc-technology/
rockets.html
A Brief History of NASA
https://history.nasa.gov/factsheet.htm
Introduction to Outer Space
President's Science Advisory Committee, March 26, 1958
http://www.plosin.com/beatbegins/archive/IntroductionToOu-
terSpace.htm
"A Selective Chronology of Defining Events in NASA History"
Roger Launius, Colin Fries, and Abe Gibson
https://history.nasa.gov/Defining-chron.htm
"Spacecraft Timeline"
The Greatest Engineering Achievements/National Academy of
Engineering
http://www.greatachievements.org/?id=3642
"Washington Goes to the Moon"
Public Radio International, series produced by Richard Paul
http://www.prx.org/series/8719-washington-goes-to-the-
moon
"Making NASA History"
https://www.youtube.com/watch?v=H5-HyE_PKZ8
NASA Center Histories
https://history.nasa.gov/centerhistories/centerhistories.htm
The Decision to Go to the Moon: President John F. Kennedy's
May 25, 1961, Speech before a Joint Session of
Congress
https://history.nasa.gov/moondec.html
John F. Kennedy and NASA
https://www.nasa.gov/feature/john-f-kennedy-and-nasa
John F. Kennedy Moon Speech, Rice University
https://er.jsc.nasa.gov/seh/ricetalk.htm

"JFK and Khrushchev meet in Vienna: June 3, 1961"
by Andrew Glass, June 3, 2009
https://www.politico.com/story/2009/06/jfk-and-khrushchev-
meet-in-vienna-june-3-1961-023278
Little Green Men
https://en.wikipedia.org/wiki/Little_green_men
http://www.sf-encyclopedia.com/entry/little_green_men
"Why Are Aliens Little Green Men?"
Mindy Weisberger, July 12, 2016
https://www.livescience.com/55370-why-are-aliens-little-
green-men.html
"6 of History's Strangest Ever Theories About Outer Space"
excerpted from Space Oddities, by SD Tucker
https://www.historyextra.com/period/6-of-historys-strang-
est-ever-theories-about-outer-space/
Queen of Outer Space
http://www.sf-encyclopedia.com/entry/queen_of_outer_space
Who Was Alan Shepard?
https://www.nasa.gov/audience/forstudents/k-4/stories/
nasa-knows/who-was-alan-shepard-k4.html
1960s: From Dream to Reality in 10 Years.
https://www.nasa.gov/centers/kennedy/about/history/
timeline/60s-decade.html
How 11 Deaf Men Helped Shape NASA's Human Spaceflight
Program
https://www.nasa.gov/feature/how-11-deaf-men-helped-
shape-nasas-human-spaceflight-program
Project Mercury Overview: Astronaut Selection
https://www.nasa.gov/mission_pages/mercury/missions/
astronaut.html
The Gimbal Rig Mercury Astronaut Trainer
https://www.nasa.gov/centers/glenn/about/history/mastif.html
Ten Presidents and NASA
John M. Logsdon
https://www.nasa.gov/50th/50th_magazine/10presidents.html
"NASA's 10 Greatest Achievements"
Julia Layton
https://science.howstuffworks.com/ten-nasa-achievements4.
htm
1970s: Kennedy Dispatches Probes to Far Reaches as Apollo
Ends
https://www.nasa.gov/centers/kennedy/about/history/
timeline/70s-decade.html
272-Telephone Conversation with the Apollo 11 Astronauts on
the Moon
http://www.presidency.ucsb.edu/ws/?pid=2133
Voyager 1 Fires Up Thrusters After 37 Years
https://www.nasa.gov/feature/jpl/voyager-1-fires-up
-thrusters-after-37
Competition vs Cooperation: 1959-1962
https://www.hq.nasa.gov/office/pao/History/SP-4209/
ch1-4.htm
NASA JOHNSON SPACE CENTER ORAL HISTORY
PROJECTORAL HISTORY TRANSCRIPT
Vance D. Brand Interviewed By Rebecca Wright Houston,
Texas—25 JULY 2000
https://www.jsc.nasa.gov/history/oral_histories/BrandVD/
BrandVD_7-25-00.pdf
NASA JOHNSON SPACE CENTER ORAL HISTORY
PROJECTORAL HISTORY TRANSCRIPT
Thomas P. Stafford Interviewed By William Vantine
HOUSTON, TEXAS—15 October 1997
https://www.jsc.nasa.gov/history/oral_histories/StaffordTP/
TPS_10-15-97.pdf
The Flight of Apollo-Soyuz
https://history.nasa.gov/apollo/apsoyhist.html
"Apollo-Soyuz: How the First Joint Space Mission Worked"
Karl Tate, July 17, 2015
https://www.space.com/29972-apollo-soyuz-space-mission
-infographic.html
"Soyuz: The Soviet Space Survivor"
Richard Hollingham, December 2, 2014
http://www.bbc.com/future/story/20141202-the

-greatest-spacecraft-ever
"The First Time NASA Docked with a Soviet Spacecraft in
Orbit"
Andrew Liptak, November 18, 2015
https://io9.gizmodo.com/the-first-time-nasa-docked-with
-a-soviet-spacecraft-in-1742930579
Apollo-Soyuz Test Project.
David Darling Encyclopedia
http://www.daviddarling.info/encyclopedia/A/
Apollo-Soyuz.html
"Apollo 13, We Have A Solution, Part 2"
Stephen Cass, April 13, 2005
https://spectrum.ieee.org/tech-history/space-age/
apollo-13-we-have-a-solution-part-2
"Apollo 13 Astronauts Share Surprises from Their 'Successful
Failure' Mission"
Andrew Chaikin, April 14, 2010
https://www.space.com/8215-apollo-13-astronauts-share
-surprises-successful-failure-mission.html
"The Real Story of Apollo 17 . . . and Why We Never Went
Back to the Moon"
Andrew Liptak, December 12, 2015
https://io9.gizmodo.com/the-real-story-of-apollo-17-and
-why-we-never-went-ba-1670503448
NASA Johnson Space Center Oral History Project,
Edited Oral History Transcript
Interviewed by Carol Butler, Houston, Texas—16 March 2000
https://www.jsc.nasa.gov/history/oral_histories/SchmittHH/
SchmittHH_3-16-00.htm

ASTRONAUTS

"How To Become an Astronaut"
by Abigail Harrison, July 29, 2015
http://www.astronautabby.com/how-to-become-an
-astronaut-2/
"How To Become an Astronaut 101"
from Lt. Col. Catherine G. "Cady" Coleman
https://spaceflight.nasa.gov/outreach/jobsinfo/astronaut101
.html
"What It's Like To Become a NASA Astronaut: 10 Surprising
Facts"
Elizabeth Howell, Space.com, June 7, 2017
https://www.space.com/37110-becoming-a-nasa
-astronaut-surprising-facts.html

GENDER, RACE, DIVERSITY, INCLUSION

Women Who Reach for the Stars
https://www.nasa.gov/missions/highlights/f_mercury13.html
"Embracing the Diversity of Our Journey: Aspirations for
Infinite Diversity and Infinite Combinations"
Former Deputy Administrator Dava Newman
https://blogs.nasa.gov/newman/2016/10/31/
embracing-the-diversity-of-our-journey-aspirations
-for-infinite-diversity-and-infinite-combinations/
"The Harvard Computers"
American Museum of Natural History, April 15, 2015
https://www.amnh.org/explore/news-blogs/news-posts/
the-harvard-computers/
"The Secret History of Women Who Got Us Beyond the
Moon" Simon Worrall, *National Geographic*, May 8,
2016
https://news.nationalgeographic.com/2016/05/160508
-rocket-girls-women-moon-mars-nathalia-holt-space
-ngbooktalk/

FLATs

https://history.nasa.gov/flats.html
Lovelace's Women in Space Program
https://history.nasa.gov/flats.html
"Katherine Johnson Did the Math for NASA
When It Mattered Most"
Michael Mink, *Investor's Business Daily*, December 29, 2016
https://www.investors.com/news/management/
leaders-and-success/katherine-johnson-did-the-math
-for-nasa-when-it-counted-most/
NASA Glenn's Historical Timeline

https://www.nasa.gov/centers/glenn/about/history/timeline
.html
Apollo 8: Christmas at the Moon
https://www.nasa.gov/topics/history/features/apollo_8.html
"Right Stuff, Wrong Sex: NASA's First Female Astronauts."
Brandon Keim, Wired.com, October 6, 2009
https://www.wired.com/2009/10/mercury-13/
Why Did the Mercury 13 Astronauts Never Fly in Space?
Amy Shira Teitel, *Popular Science*, July 17, 2016.
https://www.popsci.com/why-did-mercury-13-astronauts
-never-fly-in-space
Katherine Johnson: The Girl Who Loved To Count
https://www.nasa.gov/feature/katherine-johnson-the-girl
-who-loved-to-count
Katherine Johnson Biography
https://www.nasa.gov/content/katherine-johnson-biography
"Mary Golda Ross, the first Native American Female
Engineer"
Jasmin K. Williams, New York *Amsterdam News*, Thursday,
March 21, 2013
http://amsterdamnews.com/news/2013/mar/21/
mary-golda-ross-the-first-native-american-female/
"This Little Known Math Genius Helped America Reach
the Stars"
Erin Blakemore, Smithsonian.com, March 29, 2017
https://www.smithsonianmag.com/smithsonian-institution/
little-known-math-genius-helped-america-reach
-stars-180962700/
"Mary G. Ross Blazed a Trail in the Sky as a Woman Engineer
in the Space Race, Celebrated Museum"
Kara Briggs, Smithsonian National Museum of the American
Indian blog, October 7, 2009
http://blog.nmai.si.edu/main/2009/10/mary-g-ross-blazed
-a-trail-in-the-sky-as-a-woman-engineer-in-the-space
-race-celebrated-museum-.html
"Ed Dwight, the African American Astronaut Who Never
Flew"
Amy Shira Teitel, *Popular Science*, October 28, 2015
https://www.popsci.com/ed-dwight-african-american
-astronaut-who-never-flew
"Race and the Space Race"
produced by Soundprint and Richard Paul, Minnesota Public
Radio
https://www.mprnews.org/story/2010/04/13/midday2
"How NASA Joined the Civil Rights Revolution"
Richard Paul, *Air & Space Magazine*, March 2014
https://www.airspacemag.com/history-of-flight/how-nasa-
joined-civil-rights-revolution-180949497/?page=1
How NASA Helped Kickstart Diversity in Employment
Opportunities
Bob Granath
https://www.nasa.gov/feature/nasa-helped-kick-start
-diversity-in-employment-opportunities
"Women make up just 15% of NASA's planetary mission
science teams. Here's how the agency is trying to
change that,"
Paul Voosen. *Science Magazine*, May 4, 2017.
http://www.sciencemag.org/news/2017/05/women-make-just-
15-nasa-s-planetary-mission-science-teams-here-s-how-
agency-trying
Dr. Ayanna Howard, Animated Invention Stories
Meredith Rizzo, Madeline K. Sofia, National Public Radio,
December 19, 2017
https://www.npr.org/2017/12/19/569474169/being-different-
helped-a-nasa-roboticist-achieve-her-dream
"Meet the Mighty Women of NASA's New Astronaut Class"
Katherine, A Mighty Girl, June 15, 2017
https://www.amightygirl.com/blog?p=15516
Remarks by the First Lady at a Screening of the Film "Hidden
Figures," December 15, 2006
https://obamawhitehouse.archives.gov/the-press
-office/2016/12/15/remarks-first-lady-screening
-film-hidden-figures

SPACE AGE FASHION
Pierre Cardin
http://www.vam.ac.uk/content/articles/p/pierre-cardin/
"A Look Back at André Courreges's Space Age Style"
Veronique Hyland, The Cut, January 8, 2016
https://www.thecut.com/2016/01/andre-courreges-obituary.
html
"A History of Fashion's Obsession with the Space Age,
from Courréges to Chanel"
Ambra Vernuccio, *W Magazine*, March 20, 2017

https://www.wmagazine.com/story/space-age-style
-history-courreges

HUMAN BODY IN SPACE
"NASA's Scott Kelly Grew Two Inches: The Body After a Year
in Space"
Dr. Felix Gussone and Dr. Shelly Choo, NBC News, March 2,
2016
https://www.cnbc.com/2016/03/02/nasas-scott-kelly-grew-2
-inches-the-body-after-a-year-in-space.html
"This Is How Much Humans Actually Grow When They Go to
Space"
Claire Maldarelli, *Popular Science*, January 10, 2018
https://www.popsci.com/why-scott-kelly-grew-two-inches
-during-his-year-in-space#page-2
"Going to Space Is a Real Pain in the Back"
Ashley Strickland, CNN, October 26, 2016
https://www.cnn.com/2016/10/26/health/astronaut-back-pain
-spine-health-space/index.html
"Why Spaceflight Ruins Your Eyesight"
George Dvorsky, Gizmodo.com, November 28, 2016
gizmodo.com/why-spaceflight-ruins-your-eye-
sight-1789423059
"Space Makes Astronauts Grow Taller, But It Also Causes Back
Problems"
Jason Daley, Smithsonian.com, October 31, 2016
www.smithsonianmag.com/smart-news/space-makes-astro-
nauts-grow-taller-and-also-backs-180960922/

SPACESUITS AND SPACEWALKS
50 Years of Spacesuits
https://www.nasa.gov/centers/armstrong/Features/50_years
_of_spacesuits.html
What Is a Spacesuit?
https://www.nasa.gov/audience/forstudents/k-4/stories/
nasa-knows/what-is-a-spacesuit-k4.html
"How NASA Spacesuits Work: EMUs Explained"
by Karl Tate, Infographics Artist, July 16, 2013
https://www.space.com/21987-how-nasa-spacesuits
-work-infographic.html
Living In Space, European Space Agency
https://www.esa.int/esaKIDSen/SEM2GO6TLPG_Lifein
Space_0.html
"What It's Really Like To 'Walk' in Space"
National Public Radio, Weekend Edition Sunday,
November 8, 2015
https://www.npr.org/2015/11/08/454932716/
what-it-s-like-to-walk-in-space
"7 Things You Always Wanted to Know About Spacewalks"
Rachel A. Becker, *National Geographic*, November 5, 2015
https://news.nationalgeographic.com/2015/11/151105
-spacewalk-nasa-iss-astronaut-douglas-wheeler/
Scott Kelly Twitter Account
https://twitter.com/StationCDRKelly/sta-
tus/659857644581089280
A SAFER Way to Spacewalk
https://www.nasa.gov/missions/shuttle/f_saferspacewalk.html
Space Wardrobe
https://starchild.gsfc.nasa.gov/docs/StarChild/space_level2/
wardrobe.html
What Is a Spacesuit?
https://www.nasa.gov/audience/forstudents/k-4/stories/
nasa-knows/what-is-a-spacesuit-k4.html
"'Weightless Wonder' Makes Final Flight"
Pam Easton, Space.com, October 31, 2004
https://www.space.com/504-weightless-final-flight.html
"New 'Take Me Home' Button Could Guide Astronaut to
Safety During Spacewalks"
Loren Grush, *The Verge*, December 5, 2017
https://www.theverge.com/2017/12/5/16737728/
nasa-spacewalk-astronaut-space-suit-automatic
-return-system
"Spacewalk aborted after water leaks into astronaut's helmet"
Doug Stanlin, *USA Today*, January 15, 2016
https://www.usatoday.com/story/news/nation/2016/01/15/
spacewalk-aborted-after-water-leaks-into-astronauts
-helmet/78852104/
"Spacesuit Leak That Nearly Drowned Astronaut Could Have
Been Avoided"
Miriam Kramer, Space.com, February 26, 2014
www.space.com/24835-spacesuit-water-leak-nasa
-investigation.html.
"EVA 23: Exploring the Frontier"
Blog Entry by Luca Parmitano, August 20, 2013
http://blogs.esa.int/luca-parmitano/2013/08/20/

eva-23-exploring-the-frontier/
STEM in 30, Smithsonian National Air & Space Museum
https://airandspace.si.edu/connect/stem-30/archive

ANIMALS IN SPACE
A Brief History of Animals in Space
https://history.nasa.gov/animals.html
"Cosmic Menagerie: A History of Animals in Space"
Infographic by Karl Tate, April 12, 2013
https://www.space.com/20648-animals-in-space-history
-infographic.html
"Dogs in Space"
Nick Greene, March 18, 2017
https://www.thoughtco.com/dogs-in-space-history-3073568
"Secrets of the Smithsonian: Spiders in Space"
http://www.smithsonianeducation.org/students/secrets_of_
the_smithsonian/spiders_in_space.html
"Why Do We Send Animals to Space?"
Calla Cofield, Space.com, August 25, 2016
https://www.space.com/33823-why-do-we-send-animals
-to-space.html

MISSION CONTROL
"How Do NASA's Mission Control Centers Operate?"
Answer by Robert Frost, NASA instructor and engineer in the
Mission Operations Directorate:
http://www.slate.com/blogs/quora/2014/05/25/how_do_na-
sa_s_mission_control_centers_operate.html
Mission Control
https://www.nasa.gov/johnson/HWHAP/mission-control
Mission Control Gets Us into Space
https://www.nasa.gov/audience/forstudents/9-12/features/
F_Mission_Control_Gets_Us_Into_Space.html
NASA-Areas of Study-Human Factors and Habitability
https://www.nasa.gov/exploration/humanresearch/areas_
study/environment/enviro_human_factors.html

SKYLAB
Skylab, First U.S. Space Station
Elizabeth Howell, Space.com, February 1, 2013
https://www.space.com/19607-skylab.html
Skylab: America's First Space Station
https://www.nasa.gov/centers/marshall/history/skylab.html
Skylab: Classroom in Space
https://history.nasa.gov/SP-401/ch3.htm
Skylab: The Third Manned Period
https://history.nasa.gov/SP-400/ch9.htm
"Area 51 Declassified: Documents Reveal Cold War Hide and
Seek"
Leonard David, NBC News, November 13, 2013
https://www.nbcnews.com/science/area-51-declassified
-documents-reveal-cold-war-hide-seek-2D11591426
"Declassified Memos Reveal Debate Over Renaming the
Shuttle 'Enterprise'"
Mark Strauss, io9.com, July 10, 2014
https://io9.gizmodo.com/declassified-memos-reveal
-debate-over-naming-the-shuttl-1603073259
"Man in the News; First Black in Space"
William J. Broad, August 31, 1983
https://archive.nytimes.com/www.nytimes.com/library/
national/science/nasa/083183sci-nasa-broad.html
A History of Missile Defense, From 'Star Wars' to Trump
Bryan Schatz, January 27, 2017
https://www.motherjones.com/politics/2017/01/
donald-trump-missile-defense-star-wars/

HUBBLE
About the Hubble Space Telescope
https://www.nasa.gov/mission_pages/hubble/story/index.html
"Saving Hubble: Astronauts Recall 1st Space Telescope Repair
Mission 20 Years Ago"
Denise Chow, Space.com, December 2, 2013
https://www.space.com/23640-hubble-space-telescope
-repair-anniversary.html

COLUMBIA, CHALLENGER SHUTTLES
"STS-107: Remembering the accomplishments of the
Columbia crew"
Chris Gebhardt, Spaceflight.com, February 1, 2013
https://www.nasaspaceflight.com/2013/02/sts-107
-remembering-columbia-crew/
"Woman, 36, to Be First Private Citizen in Space: Teacher
Picked for 'Ultimate Field Trip'"
Jonathan Eig, *Los Angeles Times*, July 20, 1985
http://articles.latimes.com/1985-07-20/news/mn-5855_1
_ultimate-field-trip
"NASA's Lovely Tribute to the Teacher Who Perished
on Challenger"

Marina Koren, *The Atlantic*, January 19, 2018
https://www.theatlantic.com/science/archive/2018/01/
nasa-challenger-christa-mcauliffe/551021/
"Mission Columbia: Meet Israel's First Astronaut, Ilan Ramon"
Jim Banke, Space.com January 14, 2003
https://www.space.com/19433-shuttle-columbia-israel
-astronaut-ilan-ramon.html
Ilan Ramon Bio, Israel Space Agency
http://www.space.gov.il/en/node/981
"Astronauts and Challenger Center to Complete Christa
McAuliffe's Lessons"
https://www.challenger.org/2018/01/19/astronauts-to
-complete-christa-mcauliffes-lessons/
"Top 6 Discoveries of Cassini as Its 20-Year Mission
Comes to an End"
Ethan Siegel, *Forbes Magazine*, September 12, 2017
https://www.forbes.com/sites/startswithabang/2017/09/12/
top-6-discoveries-of-cassini-as-its-20-year-mission
-comes-to-an-end/#87fdefa39ab8

ENVIRONMENT
NASA Climate Kids
https://climatekids.nasa.gov/
How Scientists Get Data
https://imagine.gsfc.nasa.gov/science/data/data.html
"The Ozone Layer if CFCs Hadn't Been Banned"
https://earthobservatory.nasa.gov/IOTD/view.php?id=38685
"Ocean Acidification"
http://ocean.si.edu/ocean-acidification
"About Coral"
https://coral.jpl.nasa.gov/about-coral

LANDSAT
"Landsat: 4 Decades of Images and Data"
Elizabeth Howell, February 11, 2013
https://www.space.com/19665-landsat.html
Landsat Science
https://landsat.gsfc.nasa.gov/
"Happy Birthday, Landsat"
Chris Herwig, Geo Data Engineer, Google Earth Engine.
July 28, 2017
https://medium.com/google-earth/happy-birthday
-landsat-b4e91c333972
From Observing to Measuring Changes on Earth
https://earthobservatory.nasa.gov/Features/Observing/
obs_4.php
Landsat Island
https://Landsat.gsfc.nasa.gov/Landsat-island/

CURIOSITY ROVER
Curiosity Overview
https://www.nasa.gov/mission_pages/msl/overview/
index.html
"The iPhone Is Literally Four Times as Powerful as the
Curiosity Rover"
Leslie Horn, Gizmodo, August 6, 2012
https://gizmodo.com/5932148/the-iphone-is-literally
-four-times-as-powerful-as-the-curiosity-rover
Charles Bolden Speeches
https://www.nasa.gov/news/speeches/bolden/index.html
"First Black NASA Administrator Charles Bolden
'Pleaded' To Get into Naval Academy"
Morning Edition, National Public Radio, February 9, 2016
https://www.npr.org/sections/thet-
wo-way/2016/02/09/466191748/first-black-nasa
-administrator-charles-bolden-pleaded-to-get
-into-naval-academy

MAE JEMISON
Mae Jemison, Astronaut/Dancer
http://www.pbs.org/wgbh/nova/blogs/secretlife/
space-science/mae-jemison/
Five Fast Facts About Astronaut Mae Jemison
https://www.energy.gov/articles/five-fast-facts-about
-astronaut-mae-jemison
TED Talk: Mae Jemison on Teaching Arts
and Sciences Together
https://www.ted.com/talks/mae_jemison_on_teaching
_arts_and_sciences_together

LELAND MELVIN
About Leland Melvin
http://www.lelandmelvin.com/about.html
"NASA astronaut Leland Melvin's story, from NFL to space"
https://www.youtube.com/watch?v=ylf8pM8XMBY
"Astronaut Leland Melvin on His Path from the NFL to NASA"
CBS This Morning
https://www.cbsnews.com/video/astronaut-leland-melvin
-on-his-path-from-nfl-to-nasa/

SALLY RIDE
"A Ride in Space"
Michael Ryan, June 20, 1983
http://people.com/archive/cover-story-a-ride-in
-space-vol-19-no-24/

ELLEN OCHOA
NASA Astronaut Dr. Ellen Ochoa
https://www.nasa.gov/centers/johnson/about/people/
orgs/bios/ochoa.html
"Ellen Ochoa, First Latina Astronaut, Inventor and Now
Director of Mission Control"
America Comes Alive, Kate Kelly
https://americacomesalive.com/2014/09/24/
ellen-ochoa-first-latina-astronaut-inventor-now
-director-mission-control/
Ellen Ochoa
https://www.jsc.nasa.gov/Bios/htmlbios/ochoa.pdf
"An Interview with NASA Astronaut Ellen Ochoa"
Megan Sullivan, National Science Teachers Association,
January 31, 2005
https://www.nsta.org/publications/news/story.aspx?id=50189
1990s: International Flair and Understanding the Solar System
https://www.nasa.gov/centers/kennedy/about/history/
timeline/90s-decade.html
"President Clinton on America's Space Program"
https://www.aip.org/fyi/1998/president-clinton
-americas-space-program

ELLEN STOFAN
"Why Is Chief NASA Scientist, Ellen Stofan, Stepping Down?"
Ben Rosen, *Christian Science Monitor*, January 4, 2017
https://www.csmonitor.com/Science/Spacebound/2017/0104/
Why-is-chief-NASA-scientist-Ellen-Stofan-stepping-down
Ellen Stofan
https://www.nasa.gov/offices/ocs/stofan_bio.html
"Ellen Stofan Left NASA But She's Still Trying To Push
Humanity Forward"
Samantha Cole, Vice.com, April 9, 2017
https://motherboard.vice.com/en_us/article/538xwa/
ellen-stofan-former-nasa-chief-scientist
"Pioneers in Science: Ellen Stofan"
https://www.youtube.com/watch?v=KAyHYZZrGlk
"TITAN Mare Explorer: First Exploration of an Extraterrestrial
Sea"
https://www.nasa.gov/pdf/580675main_02_Ellen_Stofan_
TiME_.pdf

PIERS SELLERS
"Piers Sellers: A Legacy of Science"
https://www.nasa.gov/feature/goddard/2016/piers-sellers-a-
legacy-of-science
"Piers Sellers' Last Message"
Alison Klesman, Astronomy.com, December 28, 2016
http://astronomy.com/news/2016/12/piers-sellers-last-mes-
sage

PEGGY WHITSON
"Peggy Whitson Breaks Spacewalking Record"
https://blogs.nasa.gov/spacestation/2017/03/30/
peggy-whitson-breaks-spacewalking-record/
"Houston, Prepare for Astronauts with Disabilities"
Chris Hadfield with Haben Girma. October 8, 2017
https://habengirma.com/2017/10/08/houston-prepare
-for-astronauts-with-disabilities/

JULIA VELASQUEZ
"2017 #StudentAstronaut Contest Winner: Julia Velasquez"
Bill Watts, Xploration Station, July 20, 2017
http://www.xplorationstation.com/stories/Student
Astronaut-Finalist:-Julia-Velasquez
Julia Velasquez, Xploration Station's First Deaf Student
Astronaut
https://www.facebook.com/Julia-Velasquez-Xploration-Stations-
FIRST-Deaf-StudentAstronaut-1928981614010875/

HOMERO PALAGUACHI
"Teenager Strives To Become First Autistic Astronaut"
July 30, 2015
https://www.nasa.gov/langley/teenager-strives
-to-become-first-autistic-astronaut
"Being Different Helped A NASA Roboticist Achieve Her
Dream"
Meredith Rizzo, Madeline K. Sofia, NPR.org,
December 19, 2017
https://www.npr.org/2017/12/19/569474169/being
-different-helped-a-nasa-roboticist-achieve-her-dream

PRESIDENT OBAMA
"President Obama's Space Legacy: Mars, Private
Spaceflight, and More"

Mike Wall, January 19, 2017
https://www.space.com/35394-president-obama
-spaceflight-exploration-legacy.html
"Obama Budget Scraps NASA Moon Plan for 21st Century
Space Program"
Tariq Malik, Space.com, February 1, 2010
https://www.space.com/7849-obama-budget-scraps
-nasa-moon-plan-21st-century-space-program.html

TAYLOR RICHARDSON
"Meet Student Space Ambassador Taylor Richardson"
December 1, 2015
http://www.themarsgeneration.org/meet-student-space
-ambassador-taylor-richardson/
"This incredible teen is raising money to send 1,000
girls to see 'A Wrinkle in Time'"
Nicole Gallucci, February 21, 2018
https://mashable.com/2018/02/21/wrinkle-in-time
-gofundme-taylor-richardson/#LMuQ9UcXZkqa

ASTRONAUT ABBY/ABIGAIL HARRISON
YouTube Channel
https://www.youtube.com/channel/UCa-
bX4I5PLAu0I05gN0ZgrKw
"Astronaut Abby: Inspiring Others To Dream Big"
Jen Martin, AARP blog, April 23, 2013
https://blog.aarp.org/2013/04/23/astronaut-abby
-outreach-program-ways-to-promote-volunteering/
"Astronaut Abby Hearts NASA"
https://www.nasa.gov/audience/forstudents/5-8/features/
astronaut-abby-hearts-nasa.html

SUNITA WILLIAMS
"The Astronaut Who Brought Samosas into Space"
by Preetika Rana, *Wall Street Journal*/India Real Time,
April 5, 2013
https://blogs.wsj.com/indiarealtime/2013/04/05/
the-astronaut-who-brought-samosas-into-space/
"Space Station Suffers 'Wasabi Spill'"
Mike Schneider, Associated Press, March 2, 2007
http://www.nbcnews.com/id/17421176/ns/technology_and
_science-space/t/space-station-suffers-wasabi-spill/#.
WrfnE8gh1-U

JOHN BENNETT HERRINGTON
Native History: Astronaut John B. Herrington, Chickasaw,
Becomes First American Indian in Space
Theresa Braine, Indian Country Media Network, November
23, 2013
https://indiancountrymedianetwork.com/news/environment/
native-history-astronaut-john-b-herrington-chickasaw
-becomes-first-american-indian-in-space/
CBS Honors Chickasaw Astronaut John Herrington for
Heritage Month
ICT Staff, November 8, 2013
https://indiancountrymedianetwork.com/news/environment/
cbs-honors-chickasaw-astronaut-john-herrington-for
-heritage-month/
John Bennett Herrington—1958
http://www.nativepartnership.org/site/PageServer?pa-
gename=aief_hist_nna_johnherrington
John Herrington: College Dropout Becomes NASA Astronaut
and Walks in Space
Rebecca Wallick, McCall Digest
https://mccalldigest.com/john-herrington-college
-dropout-becomes-nasa-astronaut-and-walks-in-space/

JONNY KIM
"SEAL Tested, NASA-Approved"
Alvin Powell, *The Harvard Gazette*, July 21, 2017
https://news.harvard.edu/gazette/story/2017/07/
med-school-grad-to-trade-scrubs-for-space-suit/
"Q&A with Jonny Kim, MD, 2017 NASA Astronaut Candidate"
Lee, Student Doctor.net, July 14, 2017
https://www.studentdoctor.net/2017/06/qa-jonny-kim
-md-nasa-astronaut-candidate/

LONNIE JOHNSON
"Lonnie Johnson, the Father of the Super Soaker"
August 15, 2016
http://www.bbc.com/news/magazine-37062579
"Who Made That Super Soaker?"
Pagan Kennedy, *The New York Times Magazine*,
August 2, 2013
www.nytimes.com/2013/08/04/magazine/who-made
-that-super-soaker.html?_r=1&

WORKING AND LIVING IN SPACE
"The Psychology of Long Term Spaceflight: Music, Art, and
Creature Comforts"
Smithsonian National Air & Space Museum

https://airandspace.si.edu/events/psychology-long-term-
    space-flight-music-art-and-creature-comforts
Living in Space
https://spaceflight.nasa.gov/living/index.html
Mike Massimino Becomes the First To 'Tweet' from Space
    https://www.nasa.gov/topics/people/features/
    massimino_tweet.html
"Destination Space Station" (November 3, 2013, with Cady
    Coleman)
Travel with Rick Steves
https://soundcloud.com/rick-steves/destination-space
    -station-open
"Space Station Living" (October 4, 2015, w. Chris Hadfield)
Travel with Rick Steves
https://soundcloud.com/rick-steves/music-of-spain-space
    -station-1
"Astronaut's View of Earth" (November 26, 2016, w. Chris
    Hadfield)
Travel with Rick Steves
https://soundcloud.com/rick-steves/digging-england
"What Is Microgravity?"
https://www.nasa.gov/audience/forstudents/5-8/features/
    nasa-knows/what-is-microgravity-58.html
"5,200 Days in Space"
by Charles Fishman, The Atlantic, Jan/Feb 2015
https://www.theatlantic.com/magazine/archive/2015/01/
    5200-days-in-space/383510/
"An Astronaut Reveals What Living in Space in Really Like"
Marsha Ivins as told to Caitlin Roper, Wired.com,
    November 19, 2014
https://www.wired.com/2014/11/marsha-ivins/
"The Weirdness of Living in Outer Space"
Charles Fishman, January 30, 2015 (see also "5,200 Days in
    Space")
http://www.afr.com/technology/the-weirdness-of-living
    -in-outer-space-20150127-12yw99
"Doctor Launches 'Vision Quest' To Help Astronauts'
    Eyeballs"
Lauren Silverman, NPR.org, March 4, 2017
https://www.npr.org/sections/health-
    shots/2017/03/04/518214299/doctor-launches
    -vision-quest-to-help-astronauts-eyeballs
"Astronauts Have Done So, So Much with Duct Tape
    and Electrical Tape"
Mika McKinnon, Gizmodo.com, June 17, 2015
https://gizmodo.com/astronauts-have-done-so-so-much
    -with-duct-tape-and-ele-1711503831
Aquanauts/NEEMO
https://www.nasa.gov/feature/nasa-astronauts-train
    -deep-undersea-for-deep-space-missions

POPULAR CULTURE
STAR TREK
"Nichelle Nichols: Influence on Whoopi Goldberg"
https://www.makers.com/videos/552d3efce4b02be214c5e304
Space History Photo: Nichelle Nichols, NASA Recruiter
NASA Archives, Space.com, January 3, 2014
https://www.space.com/24147-nichelle-nichols
    -nasa-recruiter.html
LeVar Burton: discusses getting cast on Star Trek:
    The Next Generation
https://www.youtube.com/watch?v=I8aq_V2lhF8
"Star Trek's Uhura Reflects on MLK Encounter"
NPR.org, January 17, 2011
https://www.npr.org/2011/01/17/132942461/Star
    -Treks-Uhura-Reflects-On-MLK-Encounter
Actor LeVar Burton on "Geordi LaForge's" blindness
    on Star Trek: The Next Generation
https://www.youtube.com/watch?v=eT-wfcujaNE
SCIENCE FICTION
Ursula K. Le Guin
"The Fantastic Ursula K. LeGuin"
Julie Phillips, October 17, 2016
https://www.newyorker.com/magazine/2016/10/17/
    the-fantastic-ursula-k-le-guin
"Ursula K. Le Guin, The Art of Fiction No. 221"
interview by John Wray
https://www.theparisreview.org/interviews/6253/
    ursula-k-le-guin-the-art-of-fiction-no-221-ursula-k-le-guin
Octavia Butler
"Octavia Butler: Writing Herself into the Story"
Karen Grigsby Bates, NPR.org, July 10, 2017
https://www.npr.org/sections/
    codeswitch/2017/07/10/535879364/octavia-butler
    -writing-herself-into-the-story

"Octavia E. Butler, Science Fiction Writer, Dies at 58"
Margalit Fox, New York Times, March 1, 2006
https://www.nytimes.com/2006/03/01/books/octavia
    -e-butler-science-fiction-writer-dies-at-58.html
"Los Angeles celebrates Octavia Butler: A visionary
    among futurists"
Emmanuella Grinberg, CNN.com, March 11, 2016
https://www.cnn.com/2016/03/10/living/octavia-butler
    -radio-imagination-feat/index.html
THE INTERNATIONAL SPACE STATION (ISS)
"Students Talk with Station Astronauts"
https://www.nasa.gov/audience/foreducators/k-4/
    features/F_Chicago_Students_Talk_Science.html
"International Space Station: Facts, History, and Tracking"
Elizabeth Howell, Space.com, February 7, 2018
https://www.space.com/16748-international-space
    -station.html
"SpaceX and Boeing aim to take crews to the space station
    soon, but Congress has a warning"
Samantha Masunaga, LA Times, January 17, 2018
http://www.latimes.com/business/la-fi-boeing-spacex
    -capsules-20180117-story.html
"Mass. native Scott Tingle speaks about life on board the
    International Space Station"
https://whdh.com/news/mass-native-scott-tingle-speaks
    -about-life-on-board-the-international-space-station/
"13 Things That Saved Apollo 13, Part 10: Duct Tape"
Nancy Atkinson, April 26, 2010, December 24, 2015
https://www.universetoday.com/63673/13-things-that
    -saved-apollo-13-part-10-duct-tape/
"Astronaut Scott Kelly on the devastating effects of
    a year in space"
Scott Kelly, Sydney Morning Herald, October 6, 2017
https://www.smh.com.au/lifestyle/astronaut-scott-kelly
    -on-the-devastating-effects-of-a-year-in-space
    -20170922-gyn9iw.html
NASA Satellite Downlink with Astronaut Scott Tingle, '87
https://www.umassd.edu/video/2018/scotttinglenasa
    downlink.html
SPACE FOOD
Tasting Astronaut Food: Inside NASA's Space Food
    Systems Laboratory
Tested.com conversation with Vickie Kloeris
https://www.youtube.com/watch?v=6vVle67Tfjc
"How John Young Smuggled a Corned-Beef Sandwich
    into Space"
Elizabeth Howell, Space.com, January 10, 2018
https://www.space.com/39341-john-young-smuggled
    -corned-beef-space.html
NASA HUNCH Space Culinary Challenge
https://nasahunch.com/culinary-challenge/
"The NASA diet: It's food, but not as we know it"
Samantha Bresnahan & Thomas Page, CNN, February 4, 2015
https://www.cnn.com/2015/02/04/tech/nasa-diet-space
    -food/index.html
"How NASA Is Solving the Space Food Problem"
Elizabeth Preston, Eater.com, September 17, 2015
https://www.eater.com/2015/9/17/9338665/space-food
    -nasa-astronauts-mars
"Planning Menus for Mars"
Merryl Azriel, September 6, 2012
http://www.spacesafetymagazine.com/spaceflight/
    space-food/planning-menus-mars/
"First Mars Astronauts May Grow Their Own Food"
Discovery News, August 29, 2011
http://www.nbcnews.com/id/44320001/ns/technology
    _and_science-science/t/first-mars-astronauts-may
    -grow-their-own-food/#.WsPXxsgh1-U
Space Food
http://www.foodtimeline.org/spacefood.html
"Food for Space Flight: Space Food History"
https://www.nasa.gov/audience/forstudents/postsecondary/
    features/F_Food_for_Space_Flight.html
Tang, Teflon, Velcro: Are Tang, Teflon, and Velcro NASA
    spinoffs?
https://www.nasa.gov/offices/ipp/home/myth_tang.html
"Meals Ready to Eat: Expedition 44 Crew Members Sample
    Leafy Greens Grown on Space Station"
August 7, 2015
https://www.nasa.gov/mission_pages/station/research/news/
    meals_ready_to_eat
WEIRD, WACKY, WONDERFUL SCIENCE
Space Pen
https://history.nasa.gov/spacepen.html

"Fact or Fiction?: NASA Spent Millions to Develop a Pen That
    Would Write in Space, whereas the Soviet Cosmonauts
    Used a Pencil"
Ciara Curtin, Scientific American, December 20, 2006
https://www.scientificamerican.com/article/fact-or-fiction-nasa-
    spen/
"Buy the Pen That Helped Save the Apollo 11 Space Mission"
Lynn Peril, io9, March 20, 2008
https://io9.gizmodo.com/370287/buy-the-pen-that-helped-
    save-the-apollo-11-space-mission
"The Write Stuff"
https://www.snopes.com/fact-check/the-write-stuff/
"What Is the Vomit Comet?"
Elizabeth Howell, Livescience.com, April 30, 2013
www.livescience.com/29182-what-is-the-vomit-comet.html
"Mind Controlled Luke Prosthetic Arm Finally Coming to
    Market"
Lance Ulanoff, July 11, 2016
https://mashable.com/2016/07/11/luke-arm-to-market/#jRbl.
    pAkAEqr
"Warp Drive, When?"
Dunbar, Brian. NASA, NASA, March 11, 2015
www.nasa.gov/centers/glenn/technology/warp/warp.html.
"Warp Speed: The Hype of Hyperspace"
Elizabeth Howell, Space.com, December 11, 2017
www.space.com/32712-warp-drive-hyperspace.html
"3 Yemenis Sue NASA for Trespassing on Mars."
CNN, Cable News Network, July 24, 1997
edition.cnn.com/TECH/9707/24/yemen.mars/.
"NASA's Metric Confusion Caused Mars Orbiter Loss."
CNN, Cable News Network, September 30, 1999
www.cnn.com/TECH/space/9909/30/mars.metric/
"His Very Own Asteroid: Space Rock Named for Italian
    Astronaut."
Elizabeth Howell, Space.com, November 13, 2017
www.space.com/38755-asteroid-named-for-italian
    -astronaut-luca-parmitano.html
"Space Spectacles: NASA Evaluates Adjustable Astronaut
    Eyewear"
Larry Greenemeier, Scientific American, August 16, 2010
www.scientificamerican.com/article/nasa-adjustable
    -astronaut-eyewear/
"8 Star Trek Technologies Moving from Science Fiction to
    Science Fact."
Paul Hsieh, Forbes Magazine, June 24, 2014
www.forbes.com/sites/paulhsieh/2014/06/24/8-star-trek
    -technologies/#a1b88645081c
"Here's the Star Trek Tricorder That Won the $3 Million
    Qualcomm Xprize."
Dean Takahashi, VentureBeat, April 22, 2017,
venturebeat.com/2017/04/22/heres-the-star-trek-tricorder
    -that-won-the-3-million-qualcomm-xprize/
"[Infographic] See the Two Real Life Tricorders Inspired
    by Star Trek."
Qualcomm Tricorder XPRIZE. Qualcomm Foundation,
    tricorder.xprize.org/teams
"Pulmonary Pathophysiology in Another Galaxy"
Ronni R. Plovsing, MD, Ronan M.G. Berg, MD, Anesthesiology
    January 2014
http://anesthesiology.pubs.asahq.org/article.aspx?
    articleid=1918008
"Real-Life Tech Inspired by 'Star Wars'"
Tom Risen, U.S. News & World Report, December 15, 2015
www.usnews.com/news/slideshows/real-life-tech-inspired
    -by-star-wars?onepage.
"The Real Science Inspired by Star Wars"
Michael Greshko, National Geographic, December 9, 2015.
https://news.nationalgeographic.com/2015/12/151209
    -star-wars-science-movie-film/
"Stuffed animals in space: An appreciation"
Miriam Kramer, Mashable, March 19, 2016
https://mashable.com/2016/03/19/stuffed-animals
    -nasa-space-station-soyuz/#Cxlti1O0fGqV
NASA's New Shape-Shifting Radiator Inspired By Origami
January 31, 2017
https://www.nasa.gov/feature/goddard/2017/na-
    sa-s-new-shape-shifting-radiator-inspired-by-origami
"What Looks Good on Paper May Look Good in Space"
September 22, 2017
https://www.jpl.nasa.gov/news/news.php?feature=6950
"Origami Optics"
Annemarie Conte & Esther Haynes, Popular Science,
    September 5, 2008
https://www.popsci.com/annemarie-conte-and-esther-haynes/

article/2008-09/origami-optics
"Origami-inspired Robot Can Hitch a Ride with a Rover"
March 20, 2017
https://www.jpl.nasa.gov/news/news.php?feature=6782
"The U.S. Army Says It Can Teleport Quantum Data Now, Too"
Adrienne LaFrance, *The Atlantic*, June 10, 2014
https://www.theatlantic.com/technology/archive/2014/06/the-us-army-says-it-can-teleport-quantum-data-now-too/372545/
From Inner Space to Outer Space: Preparing for Your First Spacewalk
https://www.nasa.gov/vision/space/preparingtravel/innerspace.html
"NASA Will Pay $18,000 To Watch You Rest in Bed"
Maseena Ziegler, Forbes.com, September18, 2013
https://www.forbes.com/sites/crossingborders/2013/09/18/nasa-will-pay-18000-to-watch-you-rest-in-bed-for-real/#56aca5a7c558

ROBOTS
"RoboCup: Building a Team of Robots That Will Beat the World Cup Champions"
Natasha Geiling, Smithsonian.com, June 18, 2014
https://www.smithsonianmag.com/innovation/robocup-building-team-robots-will-beat-world-cup-champions-180951713/#Sw8voQGREJUdG9zk.99
"NASA may use swarms of robotic bees to study Mars"
Swapna Krishna, Engadget, April 5, 2018
https://www.engadget.com/2018/04/05/nasa-robotic-bees-mars-marsbees/?
"Marsbee-Swarm of Flapping Wing Flyers for Enhanced Mars Exploration"
Chang-kwon Kang, University of Alabama, Huntsville, March 30, 2018

https://www.nasa.gov/directorates/spacetech/niac/2018_Phase_I_Phase_II/Marsbee_Swarm_of_Flapping_Wing_Flyers_for_Enhanced_Mars_Exploration

JOURNEY TO MARS
"Mars' Atmosphere: Composition, Climate & Weather"
Tim Sharp, space.com, September 11, 2017
https://www.space.com/16903-mars-atmosphere-climate-weather.html
"The Mars Generation: Why We Must Go To Mars"
Abigail Harrison, Huffington Post, October 25, 2016
https://www.huffingtonpost.com/entry/the-mars-generation-why-we-must-go-to-mars_us_580fb785e4b08582f88c726e
"6 Space Farming Projects That Could Save the Human Race"
Lacy Cook, Inhabitat, April 11, 2017
https://inhabitat.com/6-space-farming-projects-that-could-save-the-human-race/
"Scientists Grow Super Potatoes in Mars Like Conditions"
Brid Aine-Parnell, Forbes.com, March 30, 2017
https://www.forbes.com/sites/bridaineparnell/2017/03/30/scientists-grow-super-potatoes-in-mars-like-conditions/#2691151a694f
The Mars Generation
http://www.themarsgeneration.org/

RESOURCES FOR KIDS WHO GO ABOVE AND BEYOND
NASA Climate Kids
https://climatekids.nasa.gov/
Sally Ride EarthKAM
NASA educational outreach program to engage educators and the general public with the International Space Station, STEM projects, and more.
https://www.earthkam.org/

"The Earth We Share"
Dr. Mae Jemison's international science camp for middle and high schoolers
http://jemisonfoundation.org/the-earth-we-share/
The MARS Generation
http://www.themarsgeneration.org/
Community outreach organization founded by Astronaut Abby to promote STEAM (Science, Technology, Arts, Mathematics) education and generate excitement about human space exploration, particularly NASA's plans to travel to Mars
"Houston, We Have a Podcast"
official podcast of the Johnson Space Center
https://www.nasa.gov/johnson/HWHAP
Track the ISS
http://www.n2yo.com/
NASA Education
Resources and activities for students
https://www.nasa.gov/audience/forstudents/index.html
Vanguard Stem
Web series to promote women of color in STEM education and professions
https://conversations.vanguardstem.com/
SCIVIS
Space Camp for Interested Visually Impaired Students, located in Huntsville, Alabama
http://www.scivis.org/
Astronomers Without Borders
a worldwide community of astronomy enthusiasts
https://astronomerswithoutborders.org/profile.html?id=5060

PHOTO CREDITS

acknowledgments

An abundance of gratitude to the largehearted mover/shaker/changemaker Martha Brockenbrough, who thought of me, and believed; along with the luminous Tracey Baptiste, Kelly Barnhill, Kate Messner, Laura Ruby, Laurel Snyder, Linda Urban, and Anne Ursu for their unwavering love and support. To the people of my heart, Sona Charaipotra, Dhonielle Clayton, Sayantani DasGupta, Lamar Giles, Kelly Starling Lyons, Ellen Oh, Laura Pegram, and Renée Watson, you are some of the brightest, shiningest stars in the multiverse; lifted me up throughout this process, and I'm forever grateful for your love, laughter, and true friendship—I love you. Thank you to my extraordinary agent and friend, Marietta Zacker, for her trust, light-speedy ways, and remarkable ability to inspire me. Many thanks to Anna Roberto and Erin Niumata for their steady calm and endless optimism, and so much gratitude to Nicolette Yee, Omara Elling-Hwang, Megan Luster, Sophie Amado, and Cristina Lupo for their thoughtful and diligent work to collect photos.

I am so grateful to New Jersey public school and American Museum of Natural History educator Rich Chomko, for inspiring his students to think beyond what they can see, and his willingness to answer all of my silly questions; and to my freshman year Astronomy T.A. who never gave up on me, even when things looked mighty bleak in the grade department, and was even happier than I was when the Cosmology unit turned everything around and I pulled out a B in the end.

Infinite love and thanks to Kikelomo Amusa-Shonubi, for her unparalleled research skills and sustaining cheers, Joe for listening to my endless stream of "Did you knows?!", Batman for his constant comfort and company, and Adedayo Rhuday-Perkovich for her loving, generous, and creative spirit that is always dreaming of, and reaching for, new worlds, galaxies, and universes.

INDEX